Structured COBOL Methods

How to design, code, and test
programs so they're easier
to debug, document, and maintain

Paul Noll

Mike Murach & Associates, Inc.
2560 West Shaw Lane, Suite 101
Fresno, California 93711-2765
(209) 275-3335

Managing editor:	Mike Murach
Technical editor:	Anne Prince
Cover and graphics:	Shields Design
Desktop publishing:	Ben Murach

Related books:

CICS for the COBOL Programmer, Part 1, by Doug Lowe

CICS for the COBOL Programmer, Part 2, by Doug Lowe

The CICS Programmer's Desk Reference by Doug Lowe

DB2 for the COBOL Programmer, Part 1, by Steve Eckols

DB2 for the COBOL Programmer, Part 2, by Steve Eckols

VS COBOL II by Anne Prince

How to Design and Develop Business Systems by Steve Eckols

10 9 8 7 6 5 4 3 2 1

ISBN: 0-911625-94-1

Library of Congress Cataloging-in-Publication Data

Noll, Paul
     Structured COBOL methods : how to design, code, and test your
programs so they're easier to debug, document, and maintain / Paul Noll.
             p.   cm.
     Includes index.
     ISBN 0-911625-94-1 (pbk.)
     1. COBOL (Computer program language) 2. Structured programming
I. Title.
QA76.73.C25N6395 1997
005.13'3—dc21
                                            97-4306
                                            CIP

Contents

Introduction

In the late 1970s and early 1980s, there was an extended period of (sometimes heated) debate over "structured programming"...how to define it, how to implement it, and what methods would best fulfill its promise of streamlined programming and more reliable programs.

During that period, a few dozen books were published on the subject, and more than a few promoters pushed their own structured programming methods through seminars that were given throughout the country. By the time that period ended, most COBOL shops had established their structured programming standards, for better or for worse, and the debate ended.

Today, you don't hear or read much about structured programming or about COBOL. Although that might lead you to believe that all the program development problems have been solved in a typical COBOL shop, that's far from the truth. To a large extent, programming in all but the best COBOL shops leaves a lot of room for improvement. This book is for the programmers and managers in those shops.

What this book does

The first section of this book presents proven methods for designing, coding, and testing structured COBOL programs. If you're like most programmers, these methods will help you get more done with less frustration. These methods will also make your programs easier to test and debug (which, of course, helps you get more done). And these methods will make your programs a lot easier for the next person to maintain.

The second section of this book presents five model programs that illustrate the principles and methods presented in the first section. The documentation for each model program includes program specifications, a structure chart, and COBOL code. Since one of the most important ways to improve your productivity is to reuse old COBOL code in your new programs, these model programs provide plenty of code to get you started. They also show you better ways to design and code programs.

To make this book as quick and easy to read as possible, the principles and methods in section 1 are presented with a minimum of words and a maximum of illustration. As a result, you should be able to go through this 120-page section in a few hours. As brief as it is, though, this section presents all of the critical skills that you need for improved programming.

When you finish section 1, you'll know how to apply the methods to both batch and interactive programs on PCs, minicomputers, and mainframes. Because interactive programs on a mainframe have some special requirements, chapter 5 also presents the methods you need for developing programs that use CICS. In addition, two of the model programs deal with special mainframe requirements: model program 4 illustrates the use of CICS, and model program 5 illustrates the use of embedded SQL and DB2.

Who this book is for

Because the programmers in most COBOL shops are free to use whatever development methods they prefer, this book is first for the individual programmer. Since 1977, the earlier editions of this book have helped many thousands of programmers work smarter, faster, and better on the job, and this edition is designed to continue that tradition.

Since most COBOL textbooks either omit or misrepresent professional design methods, this book can be particularly useful to recent college graduates who are entering the COBOL job market. This is also the right supplementary text for use with a COBOL textbook in a college or industrial course. Then, the textbook presents the COBOL, while this book presents the methods you need for using COBOL effectively.

If you're a programming or project manager who realizes that all isn't well in your shop, we hope that this book provides some quick and easy solutions for you too. First, when you hire inexperienced trainees, this book can provide some of the real-world perspective and training they need. Second, if your current development standards are unwieldy and unenforceable, this book can become an instant set of new standards. Unlike most of the standards manuals created in the 80s, we've deliberately cut back on the detailed guidelines so the focus is on the critical skills that need to be applied and enforced.

About Paul Noll and his methods

It seems hard to believe that 20 years have gone by since Paul Noll first came to me in 1976 with ideas for a book on structured programming. He told me that most of what the structured programming promoters were advising was "academic poppycock" that simply didn't apply to COBOL programming. He said he had mastered COBOL as a programmer with Pacific Telephone in San Francisco, and he had developed his own methods for structured program development. He said his methods were simpler, more practical, and easier to use than any of the others. "Most important," he said, "they work better in terms of productivity, debugging, and maintenance."

It didn't take Paul long to convince me that he had something special to offer, and we published the first edition of this book in 1977 under the title *Structured Programming for the COBOL Programmer*. Shortly thereafter, Paul became an independent consultant who specialized in giving in-house seminars on his development methods, and he's still available for an occasional seminar today.

At this point, it's tempting to hype this book by telling you more about Paul, his methods, and his many success stories. But I think it's better to let the methods speak for themselves. Since Paul is a simplifier, not a "complicater," I think his methods speak with a simple eloquence that will convince you to give them a try. Then, if you try them, I think the message will be clear: "Adopt these methods as your shop standards because they really do work better."

Please let us know how this book works for you

If you have any comments about this book, we would enjoy hearing from you. That's why there's a postage-paid comment form at the back of the book. If you like the way we've presented the information in this book, we'd be delighted to hear about it. And if the methods presented in this book help you work smarter, faster, and better on the job every day, we'd be even more delighted.

Paul Noll
Author

Mike Murach
Editor

```
PROCEDURE DIVISION.
*
000-PREPARE-SALES-REPORT.
*
        OPEN  INPUT    CUSTMAST
                       BRCHMAST
                       SALESRPT.
        PERFORM  100-FORMAT-REPORT
        PERFORM  200-LOAD-BRANCH-T
        PERFORM  300-PREPARE-SALES
            UNTIL
        PERFORM
        CLOSE  C  MA
               BRC


        STOP
*
```

Section 1

Theory and methods

This section presents the theory and methods of structured programming. These methods will help you develop COBOL programs that are more reliable (fewer bugs) and easier to maintain than any programs you've developed before. These methods will also help you get more done in less time using whatever measurement standard you prefer.

After chapter 1 introduces you to the theory and methods of structured programming, chapter 2 presents the methods that you need for designing structured programs. Then, chapter 3 presents the techniques and guidelines for coding structured programs. And chapter 4 shows you how top-down testing can improve the development process.

In the first four chapters, all the examples are from batch programs. But you can use the same methods for developing interactive programs. Chapter 5 shows how. It also presents some special considerations for interactive programs done in CICS on a mainframe.

Last, chapter 6 presents 10 of the questions that are asked the most in Paul's seminars and in the mail we get. The answers provide some added perspective for both programmers and managers.

Chapter 1

An introduction to structured programming

Back in the 1970s, structured programming was a much debated subject in the trade magazines and in most COBOL shops. By the end of the 70s, though, most COBOL shops and programmers had settled on the structured programming methods that they were going to use, for better or for worse, and the debate ended. Today, you don't hear or read much about structured programming; structured programming methods aren't enforced in most COBOL shops; and many new COBOL programmers are never introduced to the methods that can help them the most.

This chapter, then, introduces you to the theory of structured programming and the best methods for implementing that theory in COBOL programs. When you finish this chapter, you should have a good idea of what you can learn from the other chapters in this book. You should also have an appreciation for the benefits that you can gain from using an effective set of structured programming methods.

The theory of structured programming

Professor Edsger W. Dijkstra of the University of Eindhoven, Netherlands, has been given much of the credit for developing the theory of structured programming. Way back in 1965, he suggested that the GO TO statement should be eliminated from all programming languages. He felt that the more GO TO statements a program contained, the worse it was. He was convinced that a program was easiest to read, understand, and debug when it contained no GO TO statements at all.

To write a program without GOTOs, however, you must use other control structures. This led Professor Dijkstra and other computer scientists to give rigid definitions for the structures that are acceptable in a program. These efforts led to the theory of structured programming.

The three valid structures

The basic theory of structured programming is that any program can be written using only three logical structures. These structures are summarized in figure 1-1. They are called the sequence, selection, and iteration structures. Note, however, that there can be minor variations in the iteration structure.

A *sequence structure* consists of one or more functions executed in sequence. Each function consists of one or more imperative statements like MOVE or ADD statements in COBOL. When you combine two or more sequence structures, the result is still a sequence structure.

The *selection structure*, often called the *IF-THEN-ELSE structure*, provides a choice between two functions based on a condition. In COBOL, this structure is implemented by an IF statement. If the condition is true, one function is done; if false, the other is done. If either of the two functions is omitted (null), the structure is still valid. For instance, the function for the true portion can be omitted while the false portion contains a function; or vice versa.

The *iteration structure* performs a function repeatedly as long as a condition is true (the *DO WHILE structure*) or until a condition becomes true (the *DO UNTIL structure*). In COBOL, this structure is implemented by the PERFORM UNTIL statement. In its traditional form, the PERFORM UNTIL is slightly different than the DO UNTIL in figure 1-1 because its condition is tested *before* the function is done, not *after*. When you use the WITH TEST AFTER clause (1985 standards), however, the PERFORM UNTIL has the same structure as the DO UNTIL. Either way, you can think of the PERFORM UNTIL statement as the COBOL equivalent of the DO UNTIL structure.

Notice that all of the structures in figure 1-1 have only one entry and one exit point. As a result, a program made up of only these structures will have just one entry and one exit. A program like that can be called a *proper program*.

The sequence structure (DO)

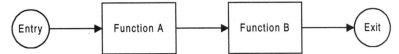

The selection structure (IF-THEN-ELSE)

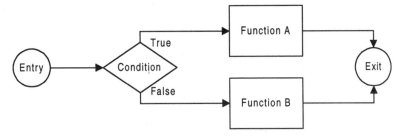

One iteration structure (DO WHILE)

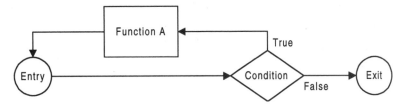

Another iteration structure (DO UNTIL)

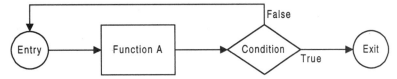

Theory

- Each valid structure has just one entry and one exit point.

- A *sequence structure* is one or more functions executed in sequence. Each function can consist of one or more imperative statements.

- A *selection structure* is a choice between two functions based on whether a condition is true or false (an IF statement in COBOL).

- An *iteration structure* repeats the same function while a condition is true (DO WHILE) or until a condition becomes true (DO UNTIL). (This is implemented by a PERFORM UNTIL statement in COBOL.)

- A *proper program* consists entirely of valid structures. As a result, a proper program has just one entry and one exit point.

Figure 1-1   The three valid structures of structured programming

Substitution and combination

To create a program, the theory of structured programming says that you can substitute one valid structure for the function of another valid structure. It also says you can treat two or more valid structures in sequence as a single structure. The result is still a proper program.

This is illustrated in figure 1-2. Here, a sequence structure, a selection structure, and another sequence structure are combined and substituted for the function in a DO UNTIL structure. The resulting structure still has a single entry and a single exit point.

From theory to practice

What a simple but elegant theory. By adhering to its principles, you can create structures of great complexity with the assurance that they will have only one entry and exit point so they will be executed in a controlled manner from start to finish. This should make it easier to read, write, and understand a program. This should reduce the number of program bugs. And this should make it easier to find and correct errors when there are bugs.

Like most theories, though, this one left many questions unanswered. How do you plan the coding for a proper program? How do you know when to substitute and combine? What else can you do to make sure you get all the benefits that this theory promises?

These questions were particularly difficult for COBOL programmers because COBOL didn't have all the language facilities needed for combining and substituting valid structures. That's why most computer scientists worked with languages like Pascal and C, not COBOL. And that's why many years passed before practical methods were developed for applying this theory to COBOL programming.

By the mid-70s, for example, only about one-fourth of the COBOL programmers were using structured programming methods at all. Worse, most of these programmers weren't using methods that made dramatic improvements in their productivity and in the quality of their programs. Today, although most COBOL programmers use structured programming methods in one form or another, there's still room for dramatic improvements in most COBOL shops.

To most COBOL programmers, in fact, structured programming means programming without GO TO statements. But GOTOless coding by itself isn't enough to make a dramatic difference in programmer productivity and program quality. What you need are improved methods for design, coding, testing, and documenting programs. Yes, the resulting programs should be proper programs, but there's a lot more to structured COBOL programming than that.

Sequence and selection structures within a **DO UNTIL** structure

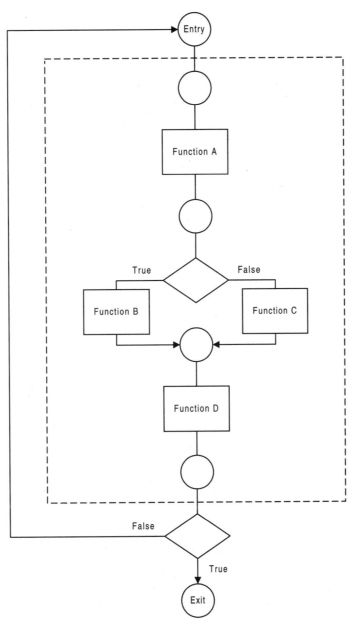

Theory

- Two or more valid structures can be treated as a single function. The result is still a proper program.
- One valid structure can be substituted for a function in another valid structure. The result is still a proper program.

Figure 1-2   Substitution and combination

Structured programming methods for COBOL programmers

The primary purpose of this book is to present proven methods for developing structured programs in CO-BOL. Those methods include structured design, structured coding, top-down testing, and structured documentation. An introduction to each of those methods follows.

If you already use structure charts and GOTOless coding, you may think at first glance that you already use the methods that are introduced next. But it's not just the use of charts and avoidance of GOTOs that determine the results that you get with your design and coding methods. What this book does is to present specific guidelines and techniques for using each method that help you make dramatic improvements in your results.

Structured design

Figure 1-3 presents the most widely used design document for a structured COBOL program. It is called a *structure chart*, and the method for developing a structure chart can be referred to as *structured design*, or *top-down design*.

When you design a structured program, you divide the entire program into modules that can be coded in a single COBOL paragraph without the use of in-line PERFORM statements. In other words, you divide a large programming problem into manageable components. As a result, this is the most critical phase of program development.

Although you can use other types of design documents as you design a program, a structure chart like the one in figure 1-3 has some clear advantages. First, you can create one quickly and easily by hand or by using a PC program like *Visio Technical* or *EasyFlow*. Second, the focus is on functions, not on programming details like what data or switches are passed to or from a module. Third, the numbers and names of the modules can easily be converted to the paragraph names that you use in the COBOL program, so the structure chart becomes an index to the COBOL code.

More important than the design document, though, is the design method. In short, how do you design from the single module at the top level of the chart to the many component modules at the lower levels? And what can you do to make sure that you end up with functional modules that are easy to code and test? Chapter 2 provides the answers to questions like these, and the emphasis is clearly on the design methods, not the design document.

A structure chart for a report preparation program

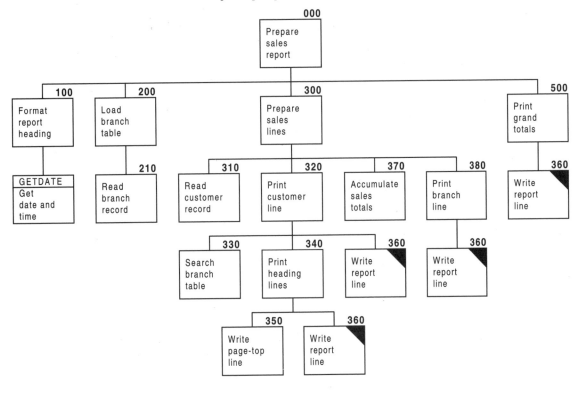

Basic principles

- Each box on the chart represents one module of the program, and each module represents a single function.
- The chart is designed from the top down by dividing each module into its component functions.
- The design process continues until each of the modules represents an independent function that can be coded in a single COBOL paragraph...without the use of in-line PERFORM statements.
- This design process provides an easy method for dividing a large program into manageable components.

Figure 1-3   Structured design

9

Structured coding

When you code a structured program in COBOL you use *structured coding* as shown in figure 1-4. Here, you can see that only the valid structures are used, so GO TO statements aren't used, and the resulting program is a proper program.

To code effectively, though, you have to do a lot more than avoid the use of GO TO statements. In particular, you need to use indentation and alignment to make the program easier to read. That way, you'll make fewer errors as you code the program in the first place. You'll be able to find and correct errors more easily when you test the program. And your program will be easier to maintain long after you've forgotten that you even wrote it in the first place.

In chapter 3, you can get our guidelines for structured coding. As you will see, they go beyond the coding in the Procedure Division. If you want to code programs that are easy to read and understand, you need to use the best structured coding principles in every division of a program.

If you want to review the coding that results from our coding guidelines, please review one or more of the model programs in section 2 of this book. There, you can quickly see how some simple coding conventions can improve the readability of a COBOL program. Although each of the model programs is a small and simple program, the coding guidelines become even more valuable as programs increase in size and complexity.

When you write programs that are as easy to read as the model programs, it's relatively easy to copy and reuse code from one program to another. After you build up an inventory of structured programs, in fact, you should be able to get half or more of the code for each new program from the code in old programs. This, of course, can have a dramatic effect on programmer productivity. And yet, this is a benefit of structured programming that most programmers and most companies don't take advantage of.

The Procedure Division code for two modules of the report preparation program

```
 PROCEDURE DIVISION.
*
 000-PREPARE-SALES-REPORT.
*
     OPEN INPUT   CUSTMAST
                  BRCHMAST
          OUTPUT  SALESRPT.
     PERFORM 100-FORMAT-REPORT-HEADING.
     PERFORM 200-LOAD-BRANCH-TABLE.
     PERFORM 300-PREPARE-SALES-LINES
         UNTIL CUSTMAST-EOF.
     PERFORM 500-PRINT-GRAND-TOTALS.
     CLOSE CUSTMAST
           BRCHMAST
           SALESRPT.
     STOP RUN.
*
   .
   .
*  .
 300-PREPARE-SALES-LINES.
*
     PERFORM 310-READ-CUSTOMER-RECORD.
     IF NOT CUSTMAST-EOF
         IF FIRST-RECORD
             MOVE CM-BRANCH-NUMBER TO OLD-BRANCH-NUMBER
             PERFORM 320-PRINT-CUSTOMER-LINE
             PERFORM 370-ACCUMULATE-SALES-TOTALS
             MOVE "N" TO FIRST-RECORD-SWITCH
         ELSE
             IF CM-BRANCH-NUMBER = OLD-BRANCH-NUMBER
                 PERFORM 320-PRINT-CUSTOMER-LINE
                 PERFORM 370-ACCUMULATE-SALES-TOTALS
             ELSE
                 PERFORM 380-PRINT-BRANCH-LINE
                 PERFORM 320-PRINT-CUSTOMER-LINE
                 PERFORM 370-ACCUMULATE-SALES-TOTALS
                 MOVE CM-BRANCH-NUMBER TO OLD-BRANCH-NUMBER
     ELSE
         PERFORM 380-PRINT-BRANCH-LINE.
```

Basic principles

- Each paragraph in the Procedure Division represents one module on the structure chart. The name of each paragraph is made up of the module number and module name.

- Each paragraph is written using only the valid structures. In addition, the PERFORM statement is used to execute paragraphs that represent subordinate modules on the structure chart.

- In all of the divisions of the program, indentation and alignment are used to improve the readability of the code.

- One of the major benefits of structured coding is that large portions of the code can be copied and reused as you create new programs.

Figure 1-4   Structured coding

11

Top-down testing

Using unstructured methods, a programmer usually wrote a program in its entirety before testing it. Then, the testing process began. At this point, though, the program usually contained dozens or even hundreds of bugs so testing frequently took longer than the time for design and coding combined. Worse, dozens of bugs were discovered after the program was put into production.

In contrast, when you use structured programming, you don't have to test all the modules of the program at once. Instead, you can use *top-down testing*. This implies coding and testing a few modules of a program at a time as indicated by the test plan shown in figure 1-5. After you code and test the modules in phase 1, you can code and test the modules in phase 2; then, the modules in phase 3; and so on until all the modules have been tested.

The advantage of top-down testing is that testing is controlled. First, you can be sure that all of the code in all of the modules has been tested. Second, when you do detect a bug, it is clearly the result of the module or modules added since the previous test run. As a result, it's relatively easy to find the cause of the bug and correct it.

In chapter 4, you can get our guidelines for getting the most from this important technique. In particular, you can learn how to stub off the paragraphs for the modules that aren't going to be tested in a run.

A test plan for the report preparation program

Program name	MKTG1200	Page	1
Program description	Prepare Sales Report	Date	11/20/96

The sequence of modules to be tested

Phase	Modules	Test data
1	000, 300, 310, 320, and 360	Three customer records: 2 for one branch and 1 for a second branch
2	Add 100, 340, and 350	Same as above
3	Add 370 and 380	Same as above
4	Add 200, 210, and 330	Two table records with one for the first branch number used in the three customer records, but none for the second branch number
5	Add 500	Same as above
6	All modules	Enough customer records to test page overflow

Basic principles

- You don't have to code an entire program before you start testing it. Instead, you can code and test a few modules of the program at a time.
- When you code and test a program a few modules at a time from the top down, you're more likely to test each of the modules in the program. This means that fewer errors will be discovered after the program is put into production.
- When you code and test a few modules at a time from the top down, it's easier to find and correct the errors. This can have a major effect on your productivity.

Figure 1-5   Top-down testing   13

Structured documentation

The primary documentation for a structured program should be the structure chart and the COBOL code. With just that information, it should be relatively easy to find the modules that you need to change when you maintain a program. All too often, though, the structure chart is neglected when a program is maintained so most structure charts don't accurately represent the current version of the program.

That's why we prefer to use a *structure listing* like the one in figure 1-6 as the final documentation for the design of a program. Here, each line in the structure listing is the paragraph name for one module of the program. The indentation shows the level of each module, and the C after a paragraph name indicates that the module is a *common module* (a module that is called by more than one module in the program). Here, the only common module is 360-WRITE-REPORT-LINE, which is called by four different modules (320, 340, 380, and 500).

Once you get used to working with structure listings, you'll see that they provide the same information that's in a structure chart. Plus, they're easy to create and maintain. For instance, you can quickly create or update a structure listing using the outline feature of a modern word processing program like Word for Windows.

A better alternative is to generate a structure listing from the COBOL source code. Then, when you have to maintain a program, you can start by generating the structure listing for the program and printing its source code. If you don't already have a program for this purpose, ours is available at a modest price. Since it's written in COBOL, you can easily adapt it to any system. And it works great…as long as the code in your structured programs conforms to the coding guidelines in chapter 3. For more information, please refer to appendix B and the order form at the back of this book.

Of course, the complete documentation for a program should include items like program specifications, screen layouts, print charts, and test run output. But it's a rare programming staff that keeps that kind of documentation up-to-date. In contrast, the structure listing and COBOL source code should always be up-to-date.

A structure listing that's generated from the COBOL code for the report preparation program

```
000-PREPARE-SALES-REPORT
    100-FORMAT-REPORT-HEADING
        "GETDATE"
    200-LOAD-BRANCH-TABLE
        210-READ-BRANCH-RECORD
    300-PREPARE-SALES-LINES
        310-READ-CUSTOMER-RECORD
        320-PRINT-CUSTOMER-LINE
            330-SEARCH-BRANCH-TABLE
            340-PRINT-HEADING-LINES
                350-WRITE-PAGE-TOP-LINE
                360-WRITE-REPORT-LINE              C
            360-WRITE-REPORT-LINE             C
        370-ACCUMULATE-SALES-TOTALS
        380-PRINT-BRANCH-LINE
            360-WRITE-REPORT-LINE            C
    500-PRINT-GRAND-TOTALS
        360-WRITE-REPORT-LINE           C
```

Basic principles

- The primary documentation for a structured COBOL program is the design document (structure chart or structure listing) and the COBOL code itself.

- Because the design documentation is often neglected when a program is maintained, the best design documentation is documentation that is generated from the COBOL source code.

- A relatively simple COBOL program can be used to generate a structure listing like the one above from the COBOL code for a program...provided that the code adheres to the principles in this book. For information about our structure listing program, please see appendix B.

- A structure listing program can also be used to generate statistics about the program that can be used for measuring productivity.

Figure 1-6   Structured documentation   15

The benefits that you get from these methods

Figure 1-7 presents the major benefits that you get from using the structured programming methods presented in this book. As you can see, each of the methods has its own benefits. From the programming manager's point of view, the end results are improved programmer productivity, more reliable programs, and reduced maintenance costs. For the individual programmer, though, the end result may be even more meaningful...the satisfaction that you get from doing your job well.

If that seems like a lot to gain from the simple methods presented in this book, please review the model programs in section 2 of this book. Are they easier to read and understand than other programs you've reviewed? Do they include code that you can easily copy for use in the new programs that you'll be writing? Does the structure chart for each program make it easy to find the module or modules that you would have to change if you were to maintain the program? Does it look like each program would be less likely to have bugs than other programs you've reviewed?

If you've ever had to maintain a production program that was written by another programmer, you know that no programs in the real world are anything like these model programs. But don't you wish they were?

Structured design

- Lets you quickly and easily divide a large program into manageable modules that can be coded in a single COBOL paragraph

Structured coding

- Helps you create a proper program with just one entry and one exit point so it will be executed in a controlled manner from start to finish
- Helps you code programs that are easy to read and understand so there are fewer errors in the first draft of the program, so it's easier to find and correct errors when the program is tested, and so it's easier to maintain the program long after it's put into production

Top-down testing

- Lets you code and test a few modules at a time so errors are easier to find and correct
- Lets you make sure that each module in a program is tested

Structured documentation

- Lets you quickly and easily prepare the final documentation for a program

The major benefits from the manager's point of view

- Improved programmer productivity because each programmer is able to get more code tested and debugged using whatever measurement standards you prefer
- More reliable programs because the programs are written with fewer errors in the first place and because the programs are tested more thoroughly by the programmer via top-down coding and testing
- Reduced maintenance costs because programs written and documented this way are easier to modify

The major benefit for the programmer

- The improved job satisfaction that you get from working smarter, faster, and better

---

Figure 1-7   The benefits of using the methods presented in this book

Perspective

The structured programming methods in this book are currently used by hundreds of programmers in COBOL shops throughout the country. These methods really do help you work smarter, faster, and better. And any COBOL programmer can learn them quickly and easily.

In the next 92 pages, in fact, you can learn everything you need to know to get all the major benefits that structured programming offers. Chapter 2 presents the essentials of structured program design. Chapter 3 presents the essentials of structured coding. Chapter 4 presents the essentials of top-down testing. And chapter 5 shows you how to apply these methods to interactive programs including mainframe CICS programs.

Summary

- The theory of structured programming states that any program can be written using just the *sequence (DO)*, *selection (IF-THEN-ELSE)*, and *iteration (DO WHILE* or *DO UNTIL)* structures. Each of these structures has just one entry and one exit point, and the result is a *proper program*.

- As you create a proper program, you can *substitute* one structure in the function of another structure and you can *combine* two or more structures so they're treated as a single function.

- When you use *structured design*, you create a design document known as a *structure chart*. In this document, each module represents one function that can be coded as a single COBOL paragraph in the Procedure Division.

- When you use *structured coding*, you create a program that uses only the valid structures. You also follow coding guidelines that lead to programs that are easy to read and understand.

- *Top-down testing* means that you code and test just a few modules of a program at a time from the top of a structure chart down.

- *Structured documentation* is program documentation that can be prepared quickly and easily. The key items of documentation are usually the structure chart and the COBOL code, but you can also use a *structure listing* that's generated from the COBOL code.

- The major benefits of structured programming from the manager's point of view are improved programmer productivity, improved program reliability, and reduced maintenance costs. A major benefit for the individual programmer is the job satisfaction that comes from working smarter, faster, and better.

Chapter 2

Structured design

When you design a structured program, you usually prepare a structure chart for it. But how do you decide when to divide one module into two or more other modules? How do you know when to stop this division process? And what's the best way to name and number the modules in a chart? This chapter answers those questions and many more.

When you finish this chapter, you should be able to design an effective program. Then, the structure chart becomes the guide for coding the program, planning the testing of the program, and so on. Since program design is so critical to the effectiveness of any structured development method, this chapter is the most important one in this book.

An introduction to structure charts

Before you learn how to design a program using a structure chart, it helps to know some of the terms that are used when working with structure charts. To start, then, you'll be introduced to the specifications for a simple program, the structure chart for that program, and the terms for working with a structure chart.

The program specifications for a simple report preparation program

Figure 2-1 presents the specifications for a simple program that prepares a report from a sequential master file of customer records. As the file is read by customer number within branch number, one line is printed on the sales report for each customer record. In addition, a branch total line is printed whenever the records for one branch end and those for another branch begin. At the end of the report, a grand total line is printed.

To complicate the program just slightly, the specifications say that a table of branch numbers and names should be loaded into the program from a file of branch master records at the start of the program. This master file is in sequence by branch number. Later, the program can search this table to get the branch names that the report requires.

If you've ever written a report preparation program in business, you probably recognize the essential requirements and logic of this program already. Whenever the value of the control field (branch number) changes, the program prints intermediate (branch) totals.

As simple as this program is, it's the type of program that gave unstructured programmers fits. And it's the type of program that can give GOTOless programmers fits too...unless they use effective methods for designing and coding the program. That's why this is a good program for illustrating some basic design principles.

Program specifications

Program name	MKTG1200	Page	1
Program description	Prepare Sales Report	Date	11/20/96

Input/output specifications

File name	Description	Format	Use
CUSTMAST	Customer master file	Sequential	Input
BRCHMAST	Branch master file	Sequential	Input
SALESRPT	Sales report	Print file	Output

Processing specifications

- The customer master file is in sequence by customer number within salesrep number within branch number. As the file is read, one line should be printed for each record in the file.

- The branch master file contains 100 or fewer records that are in sequence by branch number. These records should be loaded into a table at the start of the program. This table should then be used to get the branch name for each group of customer records.

- Sales totals should be kept for each branch, and a total line should be printed for each branch when the group of customer records for one branch ends and the group for the next branch begins.

- At the end of the report, a grand total for each sales column should be printed.

How the printed report should look

```
DATE:   01/24/1997          MIKE MURACH & ASSOCIATES, INC.                    PAGE:    1
TIME:   12:01 PM                                                              MKTG1200
                              YEAR-TO-DATE SALES REPORT

BRCH                    CUST                        SALES        SALES       CHANGE   CHANGE
NO   BRANCH NAME        NO    CUSTOMER NAME        THIS YTD     LAST YTD     AMOUNT     PCT.

12   FORT WAYNE         11111 INFORMATION BUILDERS  1,234.56     1,111.11     123.45    11.1
                        12345 CAREER TRAINING CTR  12,345.67    22,222.22   9,876.55-  44.4-

                              BRANCH TOTALS:       13,580.23    23,333.33   9,753.10-  41.8-

47   KANSAS CITY NW     12121 GENERAL SERVICES CO. 11,444.00    11,059.56     384.44     3.5
                        22222 INFO MANAGEMENT CO.  17,481.45    11,892.47   5,588.98    47.0
                        33333 DOLLAR SAVINGS BANK   5,059.00     4,621.95     437.05     9.5
                        34567 NATL MUSIC CORP.      2,383.46     4,435.26   2,051.80-   46.3-

                              BRANCH TOTALS:       36,367.91    32,009.24   4,358.67    13.6

                              GRAND TOTALS:        49,948.14    55,342.57   5,394.43-    9.7-
```

Figure 2-1   Specifications for a report preparation program

The terms for working with a structure chart

Figure 2-2 presents a complete *structure chart* for the program that's specified in figure 2-1. Other names for a structure chart are *structure diagram, hierarchy chart,* and *Visual Table of Contents (VTOC).* But in this book, the term *structure chart* is used exclusively for this type of chart.

Figure 2-2 also presents the terms that you need for working with a structure chart. To begin, each box of the structure chart represents one module of the program. If a module represents a *subprogram,* the box has a stripe across its top with the name of the subprogram in the stripe. All the other modules will become COBOL paragraphs in the Procedure Division of the program.

If a module is connected to one or more modules below it, the top module is the *calling module* and the lower level modules are *called modules.* Because a called module is subordinate to a calling module, it can also be referred to as a *subordinate module.*

If a module's primary purpose is to control the execution of the modules it calls, it can be called a *control module.* In contrast, the primary purpose of a *work module* is to do some of the work that's required by the program. The lowest-level modules of a program are always work modules, but a module that calls a subordinate or two can still be a work module.

A *common module* is a module that is called by more than one calling module so it is shown in more than one place on the chart. Wherever a common module appears, though, it has the same module number and name. To indicate that a module is used in more than one place, you can place a black triangle in the upper right corner of the box, but other graphic conventions like an asterisk after the module number can serve the same purpose.

A *chart leg* (or a *leg of a chart*) is just programmer jargon that helps you talk about a chart. For instance, modules 200 and 210 can be referred to as the load-branch-table leg of the chart. And the print-customer-line leg starts with module 320 and continues through module 360. Simply stated, a leg is just a group of modules that consists of a calling module and all of the modules that are subordinate to it.

The complete structure chart

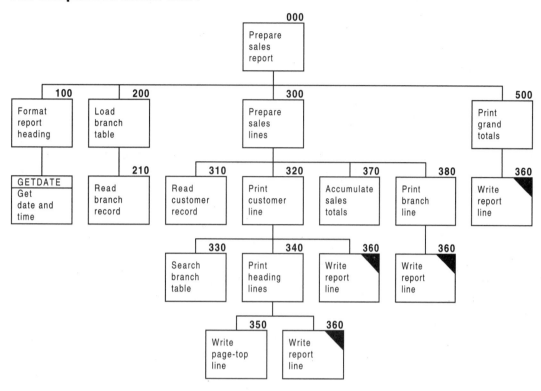

Term	Meaning
Calling module	A module that connects to modules below it (like module 000, 300, or 320). A calling module *calls* subordinate modules.
Called module	A module that is connected to a module above it (like module 300, 310, or 320).
Subordinate module	Another name for a called module.
Subprogram module	A module that is implemented as a subprogram. These modules are identified by their subprogram names within stripes at the top of the module boxes (like the GETDATE module). These modules aren't numbered.
Common module	A module that is used in more than one place in a chart (like module 360). These modules are identified by a black triangle in the upper right corner of the module box.
Control module	A calling module whose primary function is to control the execution of its called modules.
Work module	A called module whose primary function is to do work, not control other modules.
Chart leg	A group of modules that are subordinate to a control module, including the control module. For instance, modules 320 through 360 make up the print-customer-line leg, and modules 340 through 360 make up the print-heading-lines leg.

Figure 2-2   A complete structure chart and the terms for working with one

How to design a structured program

When you design a structured program, you prepare a structure chart that represents the modules that the program requires as well as the relationships between those modules. The goal is to end up with a chart that becomes a useful guide for the coding and testing of the program.

How to name the modules in a chart

The name for each module of a program should indicate what the function of the module is. To accomplish that, you create names that consist of a verb, an adjective, and a noun. As a result, "prepare sales report" is an acceptable module name, and "write report line" is an acceptable module name.

When you name the higher-level control modules, your names tend to be more general. As a result, "prepare" and "process" are acceptable verbs in modules like this. As you get to the lower levels of your charts, however, your names should become more specific.

To promote consistency in your use of module names, you can adopt a verb list like the one in figure 2-3. This list also provides some extended meanings that help define what a module that's named by a specific verb should include. If, for example, you check the suggested meaning for the verb *print*, you can see that it means "do everything associated with preparing a line for printing."

If you can get all the programmers in a COBOL shop to agree on a verb list like this along with the extended meanings, you've gone a long way toward improving program consistency throughout the shop. That doesn't mean, however, that the verb list in figure 2-3 is right for every shop. So please don't hesitate to add, delete, and modify the verbs and meanings in our list so they're right for your shop.

Similarly, please don't hesitate to suggest improvements for the module names that are used in the programs in this book. In almost any program, some of the names can be improved, and our programs are not without imperfections.

Input	Meaning
Accept	Accept the data from one interactive screen or from one field on a screen.
Get	Get edited data from a screen or a set of records.
Read	Read a record from a file; count records if required.

Output	Meaning
Delete	Delete a record from a file.
Display	Display one interactive screen or one field on a screen.
Print	Do everything associated with preparing a line for printing including (1) formatting the output line, (2) setting the line spacing value, (3) calling a Write module to print the line, and (4) resetting total fields to zero in preparation for the next group of records.
Put	Format and write a record on a file, or format and display a screen.
Release	Release a record to an internal sort from an input procedure.
Rewrite	Write an updated record on disk in its original disk location.
Write	Write a record on disk or write a line on the printer; count the lines if necessary.

Processing	Meaning
Accumulate	Add values from the current set of input records to total fields.
Add	Add a record to a file.
Apply	Apply a transaction to a record that is being updated or maintained.
Calculate	Derive new values through arithmetic operations.
Change	Modify a record in a file.
Create	Create a table or file.
Determine	Find out; may include a table search or arithmetic computation.
Edit	Check one or more fields for validity.
Format	Format the fields in a record or the fields on a screen.
Load	Read and store the entries in a table; sort them if necessary.
Maintain	Add, change, or delete records in a file based on the data in maintenance transactions.
Prepare	Prepare output by doing whatever needs to be done; for use in higher-level control modules.
Process	Do whatever needs to be done; for limited use in higher-level control modules. Caution: Don't overuse this verb.
Search	Find an entry in a table.
Sort	Arrange records or table entries in sequence.
Update	Update the records in a file based on the data in operational transactions.
Verify	Get an interactive user response to verify that an action should be taken.

Figure 2-3   Suggested verb list for use in module names

How to design the first two levels of a chart

Figure 2-4 shows the first two levels of the structure chart in figure 2-2 and gives some ideas for designing these levels. In all programs, the top module represents the entire program, and it becomes the first paragraph in the COBOL program. Usually, this module calls one primary module at the next level using a PER-FORM UNTIL statement until all of the records have been processed. In this example, the top level module is named "prepare sales report."

The primary module that's called by the top module usually represents the processing for one set of input records. For this program, the primary module represents the processing that's done for one customer record, which includes the printing of both customer lines and branch total lines. The name of this module is "prepare sales lines," which isn't much different from the name for the top-level module.

Once you've established the top module and the primary module that it calls, you can add any modules that need to be done before the primary module starts doing its work and any modules that need to be done after the primary module finishes its work. In figure 2-4, you can see that two modules are added before the primary module and one after it. The first two modules format the heading lines needed by the report and load the branch table. The last module prints the grand total lines for the report.

With few exceptions, this same type of thinking can be used for the design of all business programs. The top module of the program performs the primary module at the next level until all records or sets of records have been processed. That's why the first two levels of a program are relatively easy to design.

The primary control modules of the report preparation program

All the modules in the first two levels of the report preparation program

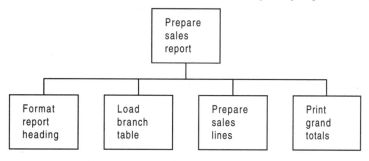

A general procedure for designing the first two levels of a structure chart

1. Draw the top-level module and give it a name that represents the entire program (like "prepare sales report").

2. Draw the primary control module that's subordinate to the top-level module. The primary control module is the one that is performed repeatedly from the top-level module with a PERFORM UNTIL statement. The name for this module should represent the processing for one input record or one set of input records (like "prepare sales lines").

3. Draw any modules in the second level that have to be done *before* any of the input records can be processed. In the example above, they are the format-report-heading module and the load-branch-table module.

4. Draw any modules in the second level that have to be done *after* all the input records have been processed. In the example above, this is the print-grand-totals module.

Figure 2-4   How to design the first two levels of a chart

How to design the other levels of a chart

Figure 2-5 presents two of the legs of the chart in figure 2-2 along with some ideas for designing the legs of a program. The idea is to create one subordinate module for each function that a higher-level module needs to do. To format a report heading, for example, the report heading module only needs to call the subprogram that gets the current date and time. So that ends the format-report-heading leg of the program.

To prepare the sales lines for a set of input records, though, requires at least three subordinate modules, or functions. One module must read the next customer record. Another must print the customer line for that record. The third module must print a branch total line whenever the customer number changes.

In this example, there's also a fourth module that's subordinate to the pre-pare-sales-lines module. It accumulates both the branch totals and the grand totals for the report. Whether or not this module is needed is debatable because these totals could be accumulated in the print-customer-line and print-branch-total line modules. In general, though, an extra work module like this helps simplify the code in other modules.

After you create the subordinate modules for one calling module, you continue the process for the next level of the chart. To print the customer line, for example, the print-customer-line module needs to call a module that searches the branch table for the branch name. It also needs to call a module that prints the heading lines whenever page overflow is required.

If necessary, you continue this process for subsequent levels of the chart. You stop when all of the lowest-level functions are work modules that don't require any subordinate functions. In addition, you should isolate each READ and WRITE statement that is required by the program in its own module. This is described next.

The format-report-heading leg

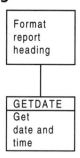

The prepare-sales-lines leg

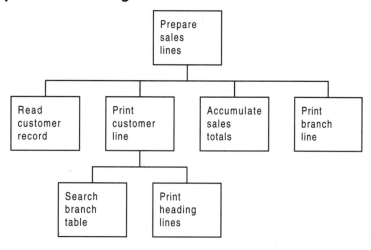

A general procedure for designing one leg of a structure chart

1. Draw one subordinate module for each function that the control module at the top of the leg needs to do. To prepare the sales lines, for example, the prepare-sales-lines module must read a customer record, print one customer line for each record, accumulate the sales totals for the current branch as well as the grand totals, and, if necessary, print a total line for the branch.

2. Use the same thought process for the next level of modules. If any of them require more than one function, draw one subordinate module for each function. To print a customer line, for example, the print-customer-line module must (1) search the branch table to get the branch name for each branch group and (2) print heading lines after skipping to the top of the next page when page overflow is needed.

3. If necessary, continue this process until each of the lowest-level modules consists of just one function.

Figure 2-5   How to design the legs of a chart

How to add the Read and Write modules

When you design a program, you should include a separate module for each READ and WRITE statement that's required by the program. Figure 2-6 explains why and illustrates the additional modules that are required by the report preparation program. One of these modules can then be called whenever a record needs to be read or written. By isolating the READ and WRITE statements in this way, you end up with a more efficient program and one that is easier to modify.

To load the branch table, for example, the load-branch-table module has to read the records in the branch master file. As a result, one subordinate Read module should be added to that leg of the chart.

In contrast, two Write modules are required to print the customer lines of the report. The write-page-top-line module writes a line after advancing to the top of the next page. The write-report-line module writes a line after advancing one or more lines. Two modules are necessary because you can't use one WRITE AFTER ADVANCING statement for both purposes.

In some cases, you include the necessary Read or Write module as a logical part of the design process. For instance, the read-customer-record module in figure 2-5 was included that way. In other cases, you have to deliberately isolate the READ and WRITE statements in their own modules. Eventually, though, this all gets to be part of the same process.

Later, when you code a Read or Write module, the primary code is the READ or WRITE statement itself. In addition, a Read or Write module is a good place to count input or output records. This is indicated by the verb list in figure 2-3.

The legs of the report preparation program after the Read and Write modules have been added

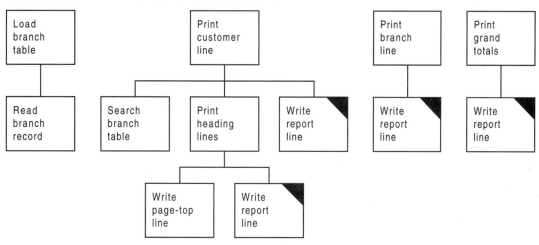

Why you should create a separate module for each READ or WRITE statement

- READ and WRITE statements are often the source of testing and debugging problems. That's why we recommend that each READ or WRITE statement for a file be coded in a separate module. Then, it's easy to locate and modify the READ and WRITE statements when problems occur.

- When each READ, WRITE, and REWRITE statement is in its own module, there is usually just one READ statement for each input disk file, one WRITE or REWRITE statement for each output disk file, and two WRITE statements for each print file. This can improve both compile and run-time efficiency.

- Since table handling operations can also have a significant effect on a program's run-time efficiency, we recommend that you put all SEARCH statements in their own modules too. Then, you can easily work with them if you need to fine tune the performance of a program.

A general procedure for adding the Read and Write modules

1. If necessary, add one Read module for each READ statement that's required by the program.

2. If necessary, add one Write or Rewrite module for each WRITE or RE-WRITE statement required by disk or tape operations.

3. If necessary, add two WRITE modules for each print file that's required by the program. The first module will print the first line on each page of a document. The second module will print all the other lines of the document.

Figure 2-6   How to add I/O modules to a chart

How to number the modules

Figure 2-7 illustrates a practical system for numbering the modules in a chart. Just start with the top module, number the second level across in large increments, and number down the legs from the third level on. As you number, leave gaps so you can add modules to the program later on without renumbering.

In the resulting COBOL program, the module numbers become part of the paragraph names in the Procedure Division, and the paragraphs are kept in module number sequence. This means that when you use this numbering system most of the called paragraphs will be found right after the calling paragraph. This reduces the amount of page flipping or screen paging that you have to do when you read a program.

Note that the numbers do *not* indicate at what level a module can be found. This too means that changes can be made to the structure chart without changing module numbers. In contrast, when more complex numbering systems are used, a change to the structure chart usually means a change to the module number, which in turn means a change in the COBOL source code.

The numbering sequence for the report preparation program

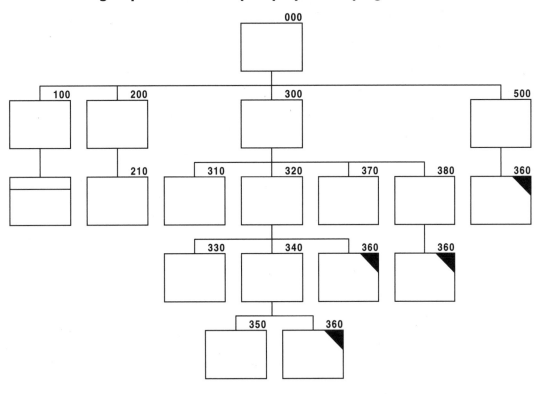

How to number the modules in a structure chart

- Use 000 or 0000 for the top-level module.
- Number the modules in the second level of the chart from left to right leaving large enough gaps for subordinate modules. If a chart is small, you can use hundreds at this level (like 100, 200, 300, and 500). If a chart is large, you can use thousands (1000, 2000, 3000, and 5000). The goal is to leave number gaps large enough to provide for any subordinate modules.
- After the first two levels, number the modules down each leg in appropriate increments like tens or hundreds. That way, you can add modules to the chart later on without changing the numbers.

Notes

- When you code one COBOL paragraph for each module later on, the paragraph name will be the module number followed by the module name as in this example: 300-PREPARE-SALES-LINES.
- In the Procedure Division, you should keep the paragraphs in the sequence of the module numbers. That way, the called modules in each leg closely follow the calling modules.

Figure 2-7   Suggested method for numbering the modules in a structure chart

How to draw charts that won't fit on one page

Figure 2-8 shows how you can draw charts that require more than one page. Quite simply, you put the number of the continuation page at the bottom of a module that starts a leg that you want to continue on a later page. Then, you repeat this module on the continuation page and design its leg. As simple as this method is, it provides for charts of many pages.

A two-page structure chart

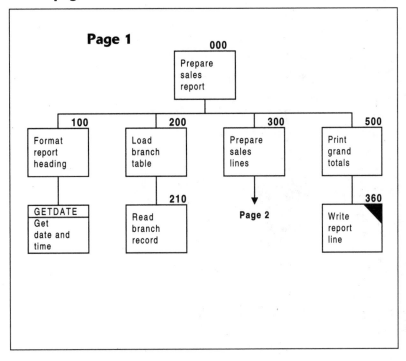

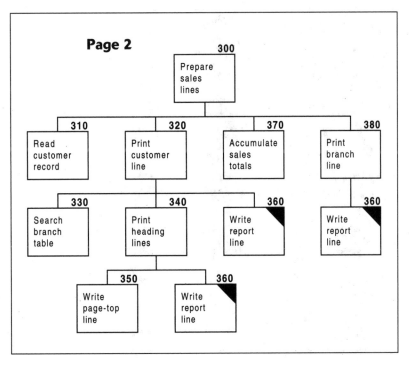

Figure 2-8　A two-page structure chart for the report preparation program

When and how to use pseudocode as you design a program

When you're new to structured program design or COBOL programming, you may have difficulty visualizing how some of the modules of the structure chart are going to be coded. That's particularly true for some of the higher level control modules. You may also wonder whether a module can be coded in a single COBOL paragraph. In cases like those, you can remove any doubts by using pseudocode to plan the code for the modules in question.

Basic guidelines for using pseudocode

Figure 2-9 presents two examples of pseudocode and gives some guidelines for using it. When you use pseudocode, it's for your own use so you don't have to follow any rigid rules. Just use what works best for you.

Simple pseudocode

```
Module 000:
    Open files.
    DO 100.
    DO 200.
    DO 300
        UNTIL no more customer master records.
    DO 500.
    Close files.
    Stop run.
```

Pseudocode plus COBOL

```
000-prepare-sales-report.
    Open files.
    PERFORM 100-format-report-heading.
    PERFORM 200-load-branch-table.
    PERFORM 300-prepare-sales-lines
        UNTIL CUSTMAST-EOF-SWITCH = "Y".
    PERFORM 500-print-grand-totals.
    Close files.
    Stop run.
```

How to use pseudocode

- Pseudocode is programmers' shorthand for the coding that a module is going to require in COBOL. As a result, you don't have to follow any rigid rules when coding it.

- In the simple form of pseudocode shown above, you code the structured programming verbs in capital letters (DO, DO WHILE, DO UNTIL, and IF-THEN-ELSE). You use just the module numbers (not the names too) when you need to refer to a module. And you use whatever shorthand you prefer for all other functions.

- If you prefer to prepare more directly for COBOL coding, you can use COBOL verbs and language that's closer to COBOL as shown in the second example above. Pseudocode is your own shorthand, so do it the way that works best for you.

When to use pseudocode

- Pseudocode is most useful when you're not sure whether the program design represented by the structure chart is going to work. Then, you can use pseudocode to plan the critical modules. Sometimes, this leads to a change in the structure chart. Other times, it assures you that your design is going to work.

- Pseudocode is also useful when you're not sure how a module on a structure chart is going to be coded (or whether it can be coded in a single COBOL paragraph).

Figure 2-9   When and how to use pseudocode to plan the modules of a program

Pseudocode for the critical modules of a program

To show how pseudocode can be valuable, figure 2-10 presents the pseudocode for the three critical modules of the structure chart in figure 2-2. As you can see, module 000, which represents the entire program, repeatedly performs module 300, which represents the processing for one set of input records (in this case, one customer master record). This continues until there are no more records in the customer master file (custmast-eof-switch = "y"). The pseudocode for the top module in most business programs is similar.

Module 300 is the most difficult module in the entire program. It uses two switches to control its processing. One switch is used to tell whether the last record in the customer file has been read; the other switch is used to control the processing for the first record in the master file. The essence of this module is one large nested IF statement that varies the processing based on four different conditions.

If you've ever written a program that prepares a report with intermediate totals, you should recognize the four different conditions. If the first record switch is on (condition 1), the program prints just a customer line and turns the switch off. After that first record has been processed, if the branch number changes (condition 2), the program prints a branch total line followed by a customer line; otherwise (condition 3), it prints just a customer line. And after all the records have been processed (condition 4), the program prints a branch line.

If you're used to avoiding the use of nested IFs because they're relatively hard to code, you need to stop doing that when you write structured programs. Yes, it's true that the pseudocode for module 300 is hard to interpret, but this is the only difficult module in the entire program. So once you get its code working right, the rest of the program is easy. The alternative to using nested IFs is to divide the control code over several modules, but that makes a program more difficult to read and debug.

Module 320, the last control module of any difficulty, also uses a nested IF statement. Its purpose is to suppress the printing of the branch name and number for all but the first customer record in each branch group. Otherwise, it just computes and moves the fields that are going to be printed into the customer line. Then, if it's time to skip the report to the top of the next page, module 320 calls module 340. After that, it calls module 360 to actually print the assembled customer line.

Does this pseudocode make it clear how these critical modules are going to be coded? After you've written a few programs this way, pseudocode like this should accomplish that goal. If you still have a few questions about how this program is going to work, though, you can review the COBOL source code for the first model program in this book.

Pseudocode for the critical modules

```
000-prepare-sales-report.
    Open files.
    DO 100-format-report-heading.
    DO 200-load-branch-table.
    DO 300-prepare-sales-lines
        UNTIL custmast-eof-switch = "y"
    DO 500-print-grand-totals.
    Close files.
    Stop run.


300-prepare-sales-lines.
    DO 310-read-customer-record.
    IF custmast-eof-switch = "n"
        IF first-record-switch = "y"
            move cm-branch-number to old-branch-number
            DO 320-print-customer-line
            DO 370-accumulate-sales-totals
            move "n" to first-record-switch
        ELSE
            IF cm-branch-number = old-branch-number
                DO 320-print-customer-line
                DO 370-accumulate-sales-totals
            ELSE
                DO 380-print-branch-line
                DO 320-print-customer-line
                DO 370-accumulate-sales-totals
                move cm-branch-number to old-branch-number
    ELSE
        DO 380-print-branch-line.


320-print-customer-line.
    IF first-record-switch = "y"
        DO 330-search-branch-table
        move branch number and name to customer line
    ELSE
        IF new branch number > old branch number
            DO 330-search-branch-table
            move branch number and name to customer line
        ELSE
            move spaces to branch number and name.
    Move the other required fields to the customer line.
    Compute the fields required for the customer line.
    Move the computed fields to the customer line.
    IF line-count > lines-on-page
        PERFORM 340-print-heading-lines.
    DO 360-write-report-line.
```

Figure 2-10   Pseudocode for the report preparation program

Three critical design principles

Figure 2-11 presents the three most important principles for effective program design. If you follow the design methods that have been presented so far, your structure charts will probably adhere to these principles. But it's worth double-checking each of the modules in your chart to make sure.

Each module should represent one independent function

As you create a structure chart, it's tempting to add a general module with a name like "do housekeeping chores" or "perform termination processing." Then, you can decide later what these modules should actually do. The trouble is that names like that don't represent independent functions, and you can't tell how your structure chart is going to work unless you know what the functions are.

The first structure chart in figure 2-11 illustrates this problem. Here, one of the modules is named "do setup functions," apparently a catchall module for whatever has to be done before the main processing functions of the program. But that sure doesn't work as a guide to the coding that's required in the COBOL program. Can you tell, for example, whether this module includes the table-loading function? Or is that function in one of the other modules?

You should be able to code each module in a single COBOL paragraph

Today, there's general agreement that each module of a program's design should be coded as a single COBOL paragraph in the Procedure Division. With few exceptions, though, this qualifier should be added to that principle: *without the use of in-line PERFORM statements*. If you don't add that qualifier, you can code large, multi-function modules in a single COBOL paragraph, which defeats the purpose of structured programming.

The first structure chart in figure 2-11 also illustrates this problem. It has four modules that can't be coded in a single COBOL paragraph without the use of in-line PERFORMs. But that just makes the coding of each of those modules unnecessarily complicated, which makes the program harder to code, debug, and maintain. This is a common design problem.

Each called module should be functionally subordinate to its calling module

This just means that the function of each called module should contribute or be essential to the function of the calling module. You can call this *proper subordination*. This is the principle that guides the design of a program.

In contrast, the Read module in the second chart in figure 2-11 illustrates *improper subordination*. Here, the Read module is subordinate to the prepare-customer-line module. Although this looks all right at first glance, this isn't logical. Although it's true that you need to read a customer record in order to print a customer line, you also need to read a customer record to decide when to print a branch line. That's why this module needs to be up one level.

Three principles for effective program design

- Each module on the structure chart should represent one independent function.
- The design process should continue until each module can be coded in a single COBOL paragraph without the use of in-line PERFORMs.
- Each called module should be functionally subordinate to its calling module.

A structure chart with one module that doesn't represent a function and four modules that can't be coded in single COBOL paragraphs

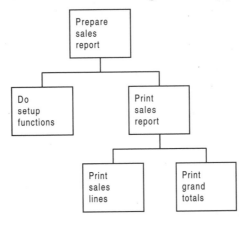

A structure chart with a Read module that isn't functionally subordinate to its calling module

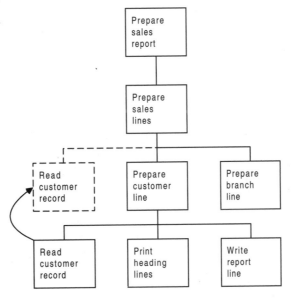

Figure 2-11   Three principles for effective program design

How COBOL can affect program design

To some extent, of course, COBOL requirements always affect the design of a program because you have to design the program in a way that can be coded in COBOL. Beyond the normal requirements, though, some statements and features have special implications that you need to be aware of. Some of the most important of these follow.

The in-line PERFORM statement

If your compiler supports the use of in-line PERFORM statements, you can use them to combine functions in a single COBOL paragraph that can't be combined without in-line PERFORMs. Since this can make a paragraph more difficult to code, debug, and maintain, you should avoid using in-line PERFORMs for that purpose.

On the other hand, you should use in-line PERFORMs when they help you combine parts of a function that belong in a single module. This is illustrated by the load-branch-table module in figure 2-12. By using an in-line PERFORM, the code for loading the branch table is complete within that single module. Without the use of the in-line PERFORM, the module for loading the table items has to be called by a PERFORM UNTIL statement that varies the index for the table.

SQL and DB2

If the data that's used by a program is in a database instead of one or more files, the structure chart for the program should have one module for each of the database operations. If, for example, the database operations require cursor control, you should have one module for opening the cursor, another for fetching the next row, and a third for closing the cursor. This is consistent with the principle of isolating each I/O operation in its own module, and this is illustrated by model program 5.

The Report Writer feature

When you use this feature, one module replaces all of the modules that are needed for printing the heading, detail, and summary lines of a report. This, of course, simplifies the design in a major way. That's why this feature is worth using if it's available on your system.

The structure and COBOL for loading a table with an in-line PERFORM

```
200-LOAD-BRANCH-TABLE.
*
    PERFORM
        WITH TEST AFTER
        VARYING BT-INDEX FROM 1 BY 1
        UNTIL BRCHMAST-EOF-SWITCH = "Y"
            OR BT-INDEX = 100
            PERFORM 210-READ-BRANCH-RECORD
            IF BRCHMAST-EOF-SWITCH = "N"
                MOVE BM-BRANCH-NUMBER
                    TO BT-BRANCH-NUMBER (BT-INDEX)
                MOVE BM-BRANCH-NAME
                    TO BT-BRANCH-NAME (BT-INDEX)
            ELSE
                SET BT-ENTRY-COUNT TO BT-INDEX
            END-IF
    END-PERFORM.
*
 210-READ-BRANCH-RECORD.
*
    READ BRCHMAST RECORD
        AT END
            MOVE "Y" TO BRCHMAST-EOF-SWITCH.
```

```
                                        200
                                    ┌─────────┐
                                    │ Load    │
                                    │ branch  │
                                    │ table   │
                                    └────┬────┘
                                         │    210
                                    ┌─────────┐
                                    │ Read    │
                                    │ branch  │
                                    │ record  │
                                    └─────────┘
```

The structure and COBOL for loading a table without an in-line PERFORM

```
000-PREPARE-SALES-REPORT.
*
        .
        .
    PERFORM 200-LOAD-BRANCH-TABLE
        VARYING BT-INDEX FROM 1 BY 1
        UNTIL BRCHMAST-EOF-SWITCH = "Y"
            OR BT-INDEX > 100.
    SET BT-INDEX DOWN BY 1
    SET BT-ENTRY-COUNT TO BT-INDEX.
        .
        .
*
 200-LOAD-BRANCH-TABLE.
*
    PERFORM 210-READ-BRANCH-RECORD.
    IF BRCHMAST-EOF-SWITCH = "N"
        MOVE BM-BRANCH-NUMBER
            TO BT-BRANCH-NUMBER (BT-INDEX)
        MOVE BM-BRANCH-NAME
            TO BT-BRANCH-NAME (BT-INDEX).
*
 210-READ-BRANCH-RECORD.
*
    READ BRCHMAST RECORD
        AT END
            MOVE "Y" TO BRCHMAST-EOF-SWITCH.
```

```
                                        000
                                    ┌─────────┐
                                    │ Prepare │
                                    │ sales   │
                                    │ report  │
                                    └────┬────┘
                                         │    200
                                    ┌─────────┐
                                    │ Load    │
                                    │ branch  │
                                    │ table   │
                                    └────┬────┘
                                         │    210
                                    ┌─────────┐
                                    │ Read    │
                                    │ branch  │
                                    │ record  │
                                    └─────────┘
```

Recommendations

- Use in-line PERFORMs when they help you code a complete function in a single module.

- Don't use in-line PERFORMs to combine more than one function in a single module.

Figure 2-12   How the use of an in-line PERFORM can affect a program's design

The SORT statement

Figure 2-13 shows how the use of a SORT statement forces another level into the structure chart for a program. In this case, module 000 contains the SORT statement, and module 050 is the top-level module of the input procedure for the SORT statement. This module is equivalent to module 000 in figure 2-2.

The get-records and sort-records modules on the structure chart represent the USING and the sort functions that are done by the SORT statement. They aren't numbered and they're marked "dummy" to show that they don't have to be coded in COBOL. Although it isn't essential that you show the dummy modules on the structure chart, this gives a clear indication of how the program design is affected by the use of the SORT statement.

In the COBOL code below the chart, you can see that the use of the SORT statement forces you to divide the program into sections. It also forces you to use one GO TO statement to branch to the end of the output procedure section when all the records have been processed. This returns control to module 000 so the program can end.

CICS for interactive programs on mainframes

If you use CICS on a mainframe, you know that this can have a significant effect on the design of an interactive program. These differences are presented in detail in chapter 5.

A structure chart for the first three levels of a report preparation program that sorts a sequential file of customer records before processing them

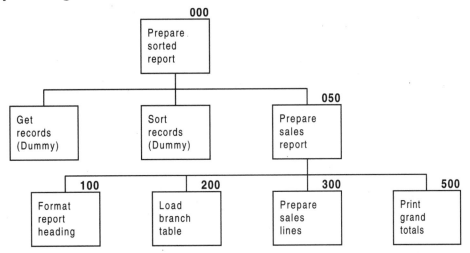

Proper use of sections and the SORT statement

```
PROCEDURE DIVISION.
*
 000-PREPARE-SORTED-REPORT SECTION.
*
        .
        .
        .
        SORT SORTFILE
            ON ASCENDING KEY SF-BRANCH-NUMBER
               ASCENDING KEY SF-CUSTOMER-NUMBER
            USING CUSTMAST
            OUTPUT PROCEDURE IS 050-PREPARE-SALES-REPORT.
        .
        .
*
 050-PREPARE-SALES-REPORT SECTION.
*
        PERFORM 100-FORMAT-REPORT-HEADING.
        PERFORM 200-LOAD-BRANCH-TABLE.
        PERFORM 300-PREPARE-SALES-LINES
            UNTIL CUSTMAST-EOF-SWITCH = "Y".
        PERFORM 500-PRINT-GRAND-TOTALS.
        GO TO 050-EXIT.
*
        .
        .
*
 050-EXIT.
*
        EXIT.
```

Some practical considerations

One of the disadvantages of using structure charts is that they're relatively difficult to create and maintain. Today, however, PC software is available that makes it easier than ever to draw and modify structure charts. In addition, there are some reasonable alternatives to structure charts.

Software for drawing structure charts

If a PC is available to you as you work, there are plenty of software programs that are designed for drawing and modifying charts. For the charts in this book, we used *Visio Technical*. Paul uses a program called *EasyFlow* to prepare his charts. And there are many other options.

When you use a charting program, you can draw charts faster than you can by hand and they're neat and clean. The big benefit, though, is that they're easier to modify than hand-drawn charts so there's less temptation to neglect the structure chart when you modify a program.

Alternatives to structure charts

If your shop doesn't require the use of structure charts and leaves the choice of the design documents up to you, there are other alternatives that are quicker and easier to use. Perhaps the simplest of these alternatives is a structure listing like the one in figure 2-14. Here, the indentation indicates what level a module is on, and a C in parentheses is used to mark a common module.

If you use the outline feature of any modern word processor like *Word for Windows*, you can prepare a structure listing quickly and easily. Then, when you want to analyze the finished listing, you can hide levels of the listing. This makes it easy for you to decide whether you've used proper subordination throughout the chart.

Remember that the purpose of a design document is to divide a program into functional modules that can be coded easily later on. So it's the structure of the design that matters, not the graphics of the design documents. If you keep that perspective, structure listings may be the simplest and best tool for designing programs and for keeping the design documentation up-to-date.

A structure listing for the report preparation program

```
000 Prepare sales report
    100 Format report heading
        GETDATE
    200 Load branch table
        210 Read branch record
    300 Prepare sales lines
        310 Read customer record
        320 Print customer line
            330 Search branch table
            340 Print heading lines
                350 Write page-top line
                360 Write report line (C)
            360 Write report line (C)
        370 Accumulate sales totals
        380 Print branch line
            360 Write report line (C)
    500 Print grand totals
        360 Write report line (C)
```

A structure listing with only the first three levels shown

```
000 Prepare sales report
    100 Format report heading
        GETDATE
    200 Load branch table
        210 Read branch record
    300 Prepare sales lines
        310 Read customer record
        320 Print customer line
        370 Accumulate sales totals
        380 Print branch line
    500 Print grand totals
        360 Write report line (C)
```

Notes

- The indentation in a structure listing indicates the levels of the modules.

- You can use the outline feature of any modern word processor to prepare a structure listing in just a few minutes. Then, you can easily reorganize the listing, and you can easily format different levels of the listing so the listing is easier to read.

- To analyze the structure in a listing like this, you can hide one or more levels of the structure when you use the outline feature of a word processor.

- For final documentation, it's better to generate a structure listing like this from the COBOL code itself. Then, you can be sure the listing corresponds to the code. (Please see appendix B for information about our structure listing program.)

Figure 2-14   A simple alternative to a structure chart

Perspective

When you approach any large or complex job, you need to break it down into manageable modules. Once you do that, the rest of the job is relatively easy. That's true for structured programming too. Once you develop an effective design for a program, you can go on to coding and testing with the confidence that each of the steps is going to be manageable.

With that in mind, the second worst mistake that you can make as you develop structured programs is to start coding without an adequate design. The worst mistake is to start coding without any design at all.

Summary

- A *structure chart* graphically illustrates the design of a program. The chart is composed of modules, and each module represents one function.

- A *calling module* (or *control module*) calls one or more *subordinate modules* (or *called modules*). A *common module* is used in more than one place in a chart.

- To name the modules in a chart, use a verb, an adjective, and a noun. This helps you focus on the function of the module.

- The first two levels of the design of most business programs consist of a top module and one primary module at the next level that represents the processing for one set of input records.

- The design process continues until the lowest-level modules no longer require subordinate functions. Then, you add one Read and Write module for each READ or WRITE statement required by the program.

- *Pseudocode* is shorthand that lets you plan the code for a module. This is useful when you want to make sure that you can code one or more modules the way they are designed.

- Three critical design principles are these: (1) each module should represent one independent function; (2) each module can be coded in a single COBOL paragraph; and (3) each called module should be functionally subordinate to its calling module.

- The design of a program is sometimes dictated by COBOL requirements. Two examples are the availability of in-line PERFORM statements and the requirements of the SORT statement.

- One of the simplest and best alternatives to the structure chart is a *structure listing* prepared by the outline feature of a modern word processing program.

Chapter 3

Structured coding

As you would guess, you use only the valid structures of structured programming when you code a structured COBOL program. But that's not near enough if you want to get all the benefits that structured programming offers. So in this chapter, you'll also learn the other coding techniques that structured programming implies.

When you finish this chapter, you should be able to code a structured program that's easy to read, debug, and maintain. Better yet, you'll be able to reuse the code of one structured program in other programs that you write. That's the technique that's essential if you want to make dramatic improvements in your productivity.

The valid structures in COBOL

You may recall from chapter 1 that the three basic structures of structured programming are the sequence, iteration, and selection structures. In COBOL, a sequence structure is just one or more imperative statements like MOVE or ADD statements; the iteration structure is implemented by the PERFORM UNTIL statement; and the selection structure is implemented by the IF statement.

In addition, COBOL provides for another valid structure, called the *case structure*. And the 1985 standards provide *structured delimiters* and *in-line PERFORM statements* that can improve the clarity of some structured routines.

The PERFORM UNTIL statement

Figure 3-1 illustrates three variations of the PERFORM UNTIL statement. The first one is normally used in the top-level module of a program to perform the primary module at the next level until there are no more sets of input records. Note that its condition is tested *before* the function is performed.

The second variation includes the VARYING clause, which varies an index or subscript each time the called module is performed. Note that this index or subscript is increased after the function is performed.

The third variation includes the WITH TEST AFTER clause, which is available with any COBOL compiler that's based on the 1985 COBOL standards. This clause changes the logic of the PERFORM statement so the condition is tested *after* the function is performed. When used with the VARYING clause, the condition is tested after the function is performed, but before the index or subscript is increased.

Coding example for the PERFORM UNTIL statement

```
PERFORM 300-PREPARE-SALES-LINES
    UNTIL CUSTMAST-EOF-SWITCH = "Y".
```

Logic flow

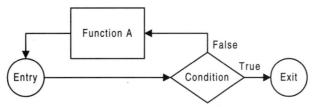

Coding example for the PERFORM UNTIL VARYING statement

```
PERFORM 200-LOAD-BRANCH-TABLE-ITEM
    VARYING TABLE-INDEX FROM 1 BY 1
    UNTIL BRCHMAST-EOF-SWITCH = "Y"
        OR TABLE-INDEX > 100.
```

Logic flow

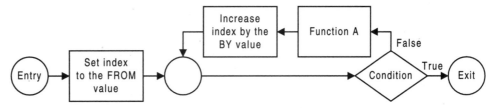

Coding example for the PERFORM UNTIL WITH TEST AFTER statement

```
PERFORM 200-LOAD-BRANCH-TABLE-ITEM
    WITH TEST AFTER
    VARYING TABLE-INDEX FROM 1 BY 1
    UNTIL BRCHMAST-EOF-SWITCH = "Y"
        OR TABLE-INDEX = 100.
```

Logic flow

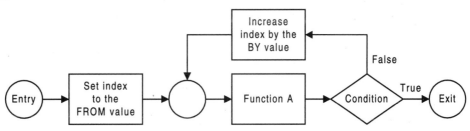

Figure 3-1   PERFORM statements   51

The IF statement

Although an IF statement by itself is relatively easy to code, structured programs often require the use of *nested IF statements* that are nested three or more levels deep. They can still be easy to code, though, if you follow the guidelines in figure 3-2.

The key to coding clarity is the use of indentation to show the levels of nesting as in the first example in figure 3-2. Here, the ELSE clause for each IF statement is found directly beneath the IF. That way, it's easy to tell which ELSE belongs to which IF.

As you use indentation, though, you must remember that each ELSE will be paired with the first IF that precedes it that doesn't already have an ELSE paired with it. So watch out. Since indentation doesn't affect the compilation, it is possible to pair IF and ELSE clauses through indentation even though they won't be compiled that way.

This problem is illustrated by the second example in figure 3-2. Here, the last ELSE clause is aligned with the first IF statement, but it will be paired with the second IF statement when it's compiled. This shows how important careful matching of the ELSE and IF clauses can be.

Guidelines

- The purpose of the indentation is to make the nested IF statements easier to read and understand...but the indentation must represent the way the statements are going to be compiled and executed.

- The indentation has no effect on how the nested IFs work. When the statements are compiled, each ELSE clause is paired with the first preceding IF clause that hasn't already been paired with an ELSE clause.

Indentation that reflects the way the nested IF statements will work

```
300-PREPARE-SALES-LINES.
*
    PERFORM 310-READ-CUSTOMER-RECORD.
    IF CUSTMAST-EOF-SWITCH = "N"
        IF FIRST-RECORD-SWITCH = "Y"
            MOVE CM-BRANCH-NUMBER TO OLD-BRANCH-NUMBER
            PERFORM 320-PRINT-CUSTOMER-LINE
            PERFORM 370-ACCUMULATE-SALES-TOTALS
            MOVE "N" TO FIRST-RECORD-SWITCH
        ELSE
            IF CM-BRANCH-NUMBER = OLD-BRANCH-NUMBER
                PERFORM 320-PRINT-CUSTOMER-LINE
                PERFORM 370-ACCUMULATE-SALES-TOTALS
            ELSE
                PERFORM 380-PRINT-BRANCH-LINE
                PERFORM 320-PRINT-CUSTOMER-LINE
                PERFORM 370-ACCUMULATE-SALES-TOTALS
                MOVE CM-BRANCH-NUMBER TO OLD-BRANCH-NUMBER
    ELSE
        PERFORM 380-PRINT-BRANCH-LINE.
```

Indentation that doesn't reflect the way the nested IF statements will work

```
300-PREPARE-SALES-LINES.
*
    PERFORM 310-READ-CUSTOMER-RECORD.
    IF CUSTMAST-EOF-SWITCH = "N"
        IF FIRST-RECORD-SWITCH = "Y"
            MOVE CM-BRANCH-NUMBER TO OLD-BRANCH-NUMBER
            PERFORM 320-PRINT-CUSTOMER-LINE
            PERFORM 370-ACCUMULATE-SALES-TOTALS
            MOVE "N" TO FIRST-RECORD-SWITCH
            IF CM-BRANCH-NUMBER = OLD-BRANCH-NUMBER
                PERFORM 320-PRINT-CUSTOMER-LINE
                PERFORM 370-ACCUMULATE-SALES-TOTALS
            ELSE
                PERFORM 380-PRINT-BRANCH-LINE
                PERFORM 320-PRINT-CUSTOMER-LINE
                PERFORM 370-ACCUMULATE-SALES-TOTALS
                MOVE CM-BRANCH-NUMBER TO OLD-BRANCH-NUMBER
    ELSE——————————————————————————— Incorrect alignment
        PERFORM 380-PRINT-BRANCH-LINE.
```

Figure 3-2   Nested IF statements

53

The case structure

In addition to the sequence, selection, and iteration structures, COBOL provides for the *case structure*, which is illustrated in figure 3-3. As you can see, this is a valid structure because it has only one entry and one exit point. Although the flowchart in this figure provides for just five conditions, this structure can be used to provide for as many conditions as necessary.

One way to code this structure is to use nested IF statements as in the first example in figure 3-3. Note the way the indentation is used and the way the words ELSE and IF are placed on the same coding line. The only disadvantage to this coding method is that you may exceed the nesting limits of your compiler when many cases are involved.

If you're using a compiler that conforms to the 1985 standards, you can also use the EVALUATE statement to implement the case structure. As you can see, you use the WHEN clause to test for each value. Within that clause, you can use the word OTHER to test for other values, and you can use the word THRU to test for a range of values like 3 THRU 5.

The EVALUATE statement can also be used to handle complex sets of conditions. For instance, this statement can be used to test the values of three fields simultaneously and perform a function based on various combinations of the conditions. This can be useful when coding the requirements of a decision table. The only danger is that this code can become extremely difficult to read and understand so you're sometimes better off using nested IFs.

A third use of the EVALUATE statement is to replace a series of IF or nested IF statements with the goal of making the code easier to read. For instance, the IF statements in module 300 of the report preparation program can be replaced by this EVALUATE statement:

```
EVALUATE TRUE
    WHEN CUSTMAST-EOF-SWITCH = "Y"
        PERFORM 380-PRINT-BRANCH-LINE
    WHEN FIRST-RECORD-SWITCH = "Y"
        MOVE CM-BRANCH-NUMBER TO OLD-BRANCH-NUMBER
        PERFORM 320-PRINT-CUSTOMER-LINE
        PERFORM 370-ACCUMULATE-SALES-TOTALS
        MOVE "N" TO FIRST-RECORD-SWITCH
    WHEN CM-BRANCH-NUMBER = OLD-BRANCH-NUMBER
        PERFORM 320-PRINT-CUSTOMER-LINE
        PERFORM 370-ACCUMULATE-SALES-TOTALS
    WHEN CM-BRANCH-NUMBER NOT = OLD-BRANCH-NUMBER
        PERFORM 380-PRINT-BRANCH-LINE
        PERFORM 320-PRINT-CUSTOMER-LINE
        PERFORM 370-ACCUMULATE-SALES-TOTALS
        MOVE CM-BRANCH-NUMBER TO OLD-BRANCH-NUMBER.
```

Here, the WHEN conditions are evaluated in sequence, and only the statements after the first WHEN clause that is true are executed. As a result, the sequence of WHEN clauses is critical if it's possible that more than one condition can be true. Is this code easier to understand than the code in nested IFs? In some cases, yes; in others, no. So you need to choose the best coding for each situation.

The case structure for the code shown below

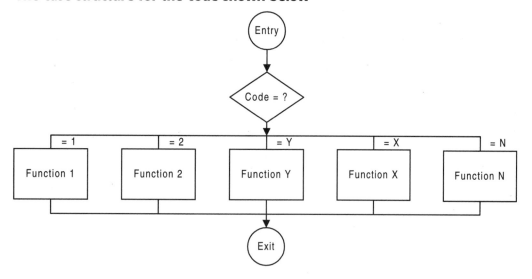

Nested IF coding for a case structure with 5 cases

```
IF TRANSACTION-CODE = 1
    PERFORM paragraph-1
ELSE IF TRANSACTION-CODE = 2
    PERFORM paragraph-2
ELSE IF TRANSACTION-CODE = "Y"
    PERFORM paragraph-3
ELSE IF TRANSACTION-CODE = "X"
    PERFORM paragraph-4
ELSE IF TRANSACTION-CODE = "N"
    PERFORM paragraph-5
ELSE
    MOVE "N" TO VALID-TRAN-SWITCH
    ADD 1 TO INVALID-TRAN-COUNT.
```

An EVALUATE statement for a case structure with 5 cases

```
EVALUATE TRANSACTION-CODE
    WHEN 1          PERFORM paragraph-1
    WHEN 2          PERFORM paragraph-2
    WHEN "Y"        PERFORM paragraph-3
    WHEN "X"        PERFORM paragraph-4
    WHEN "N"        PERFORM paragraph-5
    WHEN OTHER      MOVE "N" TO VALID-TRAN-SWITCH
                    ADD 1 TO INVALID-TRAN-COUNT.
```

Note

- The EVALUATE statement is a powerful statement that can be used instead of a series of IF statements. In many cases, its use can make the code easier to read and understand. This is illustrated by the top module in the code for model program 4.

Figure 3-3   The case structure

55

Structured delimiters

If you're using a COBOL compiler that supports the 1985 standards, you can use *structured delimiters* with the verbs listed in figure 3-4. A structured delimiter is simply END- followed by the verb name as in END-IF. Delimiters like this are useful when you're coding one statement within another one. This is illustrated by the examples in this figure.

In the first example, the END-COMPUTE delimiter is used to end a COMPUTE statement that's coded within an IF statement. If the delimiter wasn't available, the statement following the delimiter would be treated as part of the ON SIZE ERROR clause, and you couldn't code this function as easily.

The in-line PERFORM statement

The *in-line PERFORM* statement is a structure that many structured programming advocates have wanted for years. It became available with compilers that support the 1985 COBOL standards, and this statement is illustrated in the second example in figure 3-4.

When you code an in-line PERFORM, the performed function comes right after the PERFORM statement, and you end the function with the END-PERFORM delimiter. In other words, the performed function is not coded in a separate paragraph. In the second example in figure 3-4, the in-line PERFORM statement uses the WITH TEST AFTER clause, and an END-IF delimiter is used to end the IF statement within the in-line PERFORM.

The problem with the in-line PERFORM statement is that it makes it relatively easy for you to code more than one function as a single COBOL paragraph. Since this makes a module more difficult to read, debug, and maintain, you should avoid the use of these statements when they combine more than one function. On the other hand, you should use them when they help you code a single function in a single paragraph as shown in this example.

Guidelines

- Use structured delimiters whenever they help simplify coding.
- Use in-line PERFORM statements whenever they help you code a single function in a single COBOL paragraph.
- Don't use in-line PERFORM statements to combine two or more functions in a single paragraph.

The verb list for structured delimiters

READ	ADD	PERFORM
WRITE	SUBTRACT	IF
REWRITE	MULTIPLY	EVALUATE
DELETE	DIVIDE	SEARCH
RETURN	COMPUTE	CALL
START	UNSTRING	STRING

An IF statement that makes effective use of the END-COMPUTE delimiter

```
IF CM-SALES-LAST-YTD NOT EQUAL ZERO
    COMPUTE CHANGE-PERCENT ROUNDED =
        CHANGE-AMOUNT / CM-SALES-LAST-YTD * 100
            ON SIZE ERROR
                MOVE "OVRFLW" TO CL-CHANGE-PERCENT-R
    END-COMPUTE
    MOVE CHANGE-PERCENT TO CL-CHANGE-PERCENT
ELSE
    MOVE "  N/A" TO CL-CHANGE-PERCENT-R.
```

A load-table module that makes effective use of structured delimiters and an in-line PERFORM statement

```
200-LOAD-BRANCH-TABLE.
*
    PERFORM
        WITH TEST AFTER
        VARYING BT-INDEX FROM 1 BY 1
            UNTIL BRCHMAST-EOF
            OR BT-INDEX = 100
        PERFORM 210-READ-BRANCH-RECORD ────┐
        IF NOT BRCHMAST-EOF                 │
            MOVE BM-BRANCH-NUMBER           │
                TO BT-BRANCH-NUMBER (BT-INDEX)
            MOVE BM-BRANCH-NAME             │── In-line statements
                TO BT-BRANCH-NAME (BT-INDEX)
        ELSE                                │
            SET BT-ENTRY-COUNT TO BT-INDEX  │
        END-IF ─────────────────────────────┘
    END-PERFORM.
```

Figure 3-4 Structured delimiters and in-line PERFORM statements

Coding conventions

Coding conventions, or shop standards, are the coding rules and guidelines that the programmers in a COBOL shop agree to follow. In many shops, however, these conventions are so detailed and numerous that they are difficult to follow and enforce. As a result, the programmers ignore most of the conventions, and there is little consistency or standardization from one program to another.

What follows, then, is a set of conventions that are easy to remember and follow if you're a programmer and easy to review and enforce if you're a manager. If all of the programmers in a shop follow these conventions, all of the new programs in a shop will start to have a standard appearance. After a few years, this can have a significant effect on the time and expense that's spent on program maintenance.

General coding conventions

In all four divisions of a program, you should use indentation and blank lines to make the program easier to read. Whenever compiler efficiency matters, though, we recommend the use of *blank comment lines*, not completely blank lines. Since blank comment lines have an asterisk (*) in column 7, they are ignored by the compiler. In general, PC compilers are so fast that this doesn't matter, but on a mainframe that's handling the compilations of dozens of programmers, it's worth taking the extra time to type these asterisks.

Data Division conventions

Figure 3-5 gives a simple set of conventions for the Data Division and illustrates their use. If you group data items to show their relationships, you won't need 77 levels and you can code the usage for some groups at the 01 level. If you code the groups in the same sequences in each program that you write, you'll be able to find the data items more quickly. And if you use condition names, the coding in the Procedure Division is simplified later on.

As for data names, of course, they should be meaningful. That's been encouraged for years. But you still find data names like BOB, X1, MTN, SUB, and much worse in new programs. So if you want to get all the benefits of structured programming, don't save keystrokes by abbreviating the words you use in data names. If necessary, use all of the thirty characters that COBOL allows.

When fields are all part of the same record, show the relationships by giving the same two- or three-character prefix to all fields in the record. If you're coding a routine that directly relates to a user function, use the same names that the user uses. And use the same names for the same types of fields in all your programs.

The more meaningful your names are, of course, the easier it is to remember the names you've used when you code the Procedure Division, and the easier it is for someone else to read and maintain your program later on. As simple as this notion is, poor data names are a major weakness in most COBOL programs.

Data Division conventions

- Use blank lines and indentation to improve readability. (If compile time matters, you should use *blank comment lines*, not completely blank lines.)

- Group related data items so it's easier to find the items you're looking for.

- Use a consistent sequence of entries in the Working-Storage Section of all of your programs. Suggested sequence: (1) switches, (2) flags, (3) print fields, (4) date and time fields, (5) count fields, (6) total fields, (7) other work fields, (8) tables, (9) record descriptions for input or output files, (10) heading line descriptions for print files, (11) detail or body line descriptions for print files, and (12) total line descriptions for print files.

- Use condition names for switch and flag settings.

- Use meaningful data names!!!

Data Division code that illustrates these conventions

```
WORKING-STORAGE SECTION.
*
 01  SWITCHES.
*
    05  FIRST-RECORD-SWITCH       PIC X              VALUE "Y".
        88  FIRST-RECORD                             VALUE "Y".
    05  CUSTMAST-EOF-SWITCH       PIC X              VALUE "N".
        88  CUSTMAST-EOF                             VALUE "Y".
    05  BRCHMAST-EOF-SWITCH       PIC X              VALUE "N".
        88  BRCHMAST-EOF                             VALUE "Y".
*
 01  PRINT-FIELDS              PACKED-DECIMAL.
*
    05  SPACE-CONTROL            PIC S9.
    05  PAGE-COUNT              PIC S9(3)         VALUE ZERO.
    05  LINES-ON-PAGE          PIC S9(3)         VALUE +53.
    05  LINE-COUNT             PIC S9(3)         VALUE +99.
*
 01  TOTAL-FIELDS             PACKED-DECIMAL.
*
    05  BRANCH-TOTAL-THIS-YTD  PIC S9(7)V99      VALUE ZERO.
    05  BRANCH-TOTAL-LAST-YTD  PIC S9(7)V99      VALUE ZERO.
    05  GRAND-TOTAL-THIS-YTD   PIC S9(9)V99      VALUE ZERO.
    05  GRAND-TOTAL-LAST-YTD   PIC S9(9)V99      VALUE ZERO.
*
 01  WORK-FIELDS.
*
    05  OLD-BRANCH-NUMBER  PIC XX.
    05  BRANCH-NAME        PIC X(18).
    05  CHANGE-AMOUNT      PIC S9(7)V99  VALUE ZERO  PACKED-DECIMAL.
    05  CHANGE-PERCENT     PIC S9(3)V99  VALUE ZERO  PACKED-DECIMAL.
*
 01  BRANCH-TABLE.
*
    05  BT-ENTRIES              OCCURS 100 TIMES
                                INDEXED BY BT-INDEX.
        10  BT-BRANCH-NUMBER    PIC XX.
        10  BT-BRANCH-NAME      PIC X(18).
    05  BT-ENTRY-COUNT          INDEX.
```

Figure 3-5   Data Division conventions

59

Procedure Division conventions

Figure 3-6 presents a simple set of conventions for the Procedure Division that are illustrated throughout this book. When you code this way, each paragraph is relatively easy to read, debug, and maintain. Note, however, that the readability also depends on the use of meaningful data names in the Data Division. If the data names aren't meaningful, the Procedure Division code gets to be much harder to read.

Although it's best to code each module on the structure chart as one paragraph in the Procedure Division, COBOL sometimes forces you to use sections. This happens when you use the SORT statement as shown in figure 2-13 of the last chapter. This happens when you use certain CICS statements for interactive programs on a mainframe as explained in chapter 5. And this happens when you use Declaratives.

When COBOL forces you to use sections, you can still get all the benefits of structured programming if you adopt some logical conventions for using sections. In figure 2-13, for example, you can see our conventions for using the sections that are required by the use of the SORT statement. If necessary, similar accommodations can be made for other uses of sections.

One debate that sometimes starts when talking about coding standards for the Procedure Division concerns the use periods. Those in one group say that you shouldn't use periods after the statements in the Procedure Division because an accidental period in the wrong place can cause a serious debugging problem. Instead, this group says, you should use structured delimiters (like END-IF and END-PERFORM) to end those statements that need to be ended. Those in the other group say that a period is also a delimiter that ends statements so all you need to do is be careful when you use them. These people say that you should only use structured delimiters when you need them.

In this book, all of the examples use periods because that's what we're used to. But this is one of those considerations that doesn't have to be a part of a shop's standards. As long as the code in a program is clear, the programmer's coding preferences don't matter much.

Procedure Division conventions

- Use blank lines and indentation to improve readability. (If compile time matters, you should use *blank comment lines*, not completely blank lines.)

- Use only the statements that represent valid structures. (Don't use GO TO statements.)

- Code each module on the structure chart with a single COBOL paragraph.

- Create the paragraph names from the structure chart by combining the module numbers with the module names as in 000-PREPARE-SALES-REPORT. If a resulting name is more than 30 characters, shorten one or more of the words in the module name.

- Keep the paragraphs in sequence by module number.

- Use condition names to improve clarity.

- Don't use PERFORM THRU statements, and don't use sections unless COBOL requires their use.

A module that uses condition names and the module that sets the switch for one of the conditions

```
300-PREPARE-SALES-LINES.
*
    PERFORM 310-READ-CUSTOMER-RECORD.
    IF NOT CUSTMAST-EOF
        IF FIRST-RECORD
            MOVE CM-BRANCH-NUMBER TO OLD-BRANCH-NUMBER
            PERFORM 320-PRINT-CUSTOMER-LINE
            PERFORM 370-ACCUMULATE-SALES-TOTALS
            MOVE "N" TO FIRST-RECORD-SWITCH
        ELSE
            IF CM-BRANCH-NUMBER = OLD-BRANCH-NUMBER
                PERFORM 320-PRINT-CUSTOMER-LINE
                PERFORM 370-ACCUMULATE-SALES-TOTALS
            ELSE
                PERFORM 380-PRINT-BRANCH-LINE
                PERFORM 320-PRINT-CUSTOMER-LINE
                PERFORM 370-ACCUMULATE-SALES-TOTALS
                MOVE CM-BRANCH-NUMBER TO OLD-BRANCH-NUMBER
    ELSE
        PERFORM 380-PRINT-BRANCH-LINE.
*
310-READ-CUSTOMER-RECORD.
*
    READ CUSTMAST
        AT END
            MOVE "Y" TO CUSTMAST-EOF-SWITCH.
```

Figure 3-6   Procedure Division conventions

Three critical coding principles

If you follow all of the guidelines and conventions presented thus far, you will be a better programmer. But you still may not get the major benefits that structured programming promises. Here, then, are three critical principles that will help you make dramatic improvements in productivity at the same time that you make your programs easier to read, debug, and maintain.

Always reuse old code in new programs

Figure 3-7 presents the most important principle for improving programming productivity. When you reuse old code in new programs, your productivity soars because you spend less time entering code, less time compiling (fewer diagnostics), and less time testing (fewer bugs).

In general, there are three ways that you can reuse old code in new programs. First, you should start each new program from an old program that does similar functions. Then, you can delete the lines that you don't need and modify the lines that you do need. That way, you can quickly establish the first few hundred lines of a new program, including code for all four divisions of the program.

Second, you can copy code from old programs whenever your new program requires a similar function. If, for example, your program requires that a table be loaded at the start of the program and searched later on, you can copy portions of the code that does those functions from another program. This includes the code in the Data Division as well as the code in the Procedure Division. After you copy the code into your program, you can delete the lines you don't need and modify the other lines as needed.

Third, you can reuse code by using COPY members. This is valuable in the Data Division where COPY members should be used for the record descriptions in all files and for repeated use of descriptions like those for heading lines, date fields, and time fields. In contrast, the use of COPY members in the Procedure Division is usually more trouble than it's worth. Instead, it's easier to copy the code you want to use from some other program and modify that code as needed.

When you use these methods to reuse old code in new programs, you can often develop half or more of a new program from old code. This, of course, can have a dramatic effect on your productivity. To get the most from this principle, though, you need to develop modules that are both independent and easy to understand. That makes the modules easy to reuse.

Guidelines

- Start each new program from an old program with similar requirements.
- Copy the code from an old program whenever your program requires a similar function.
- Always use the COPY members that are available for your program.

Reusable code for a top-level module

```
000-PREPARE-SALES-REPORT.
*
    OPEN INPUT  CUSTMAST
                BRCHMAST
         OUTPUT SALESRPT.
    PERFORM 100-FORMAT-REPORT-HEADING.
    PERFORM 200-LOAD-BRANCH-TABLE.
    PERFORM 300-PREPARE-SALES-LINES
        UNTIL CUSTMAST-EOF.
    PERFORM 500-PRINT-GRAND-TOTALS.
    CLOSE CUSTMAST
          BRCHMAST
          SALESRPT.
    STOP RUN.
```

Reusable code for formatting a report heading

```
100-FORMAT-REPORT-HEADING.
*
    CALL "GETDATE" USING TODAYS-DATE TODAYS-TIME.
    MOVE TODAYS-DATE   TO HDG1-DATE.
    MOVE TODAYS-TIME   TO HDG2-TIME.
    MOVE "MKTG1200"    TO HDG2-REPORT-NUMBER.
    MOVE REPORT-TITLE  TO HDG3-REPORT-TITLE.
```

Reusable code for searching a one-level table

```
330-SEARCH-BRANCH-TABLE.
*
    SET BT-INDEX TO 1.
    SEARCH BT-ENTRIES
        AT END
            MOVE "BRANCH NOT FOUND" TO BRANCH-NAME
        WHEN BT-BRANCH-NUMBER (BT-INDEX) = CM-BRANCH-NUMBER
            MOVE BT-BRANCH-NAME (BT-INDEX) TO BRANCH-NAME
        WHEN BT-INDEX > BT-ENTRY-COUNT
            MOVE "BRANCH NOT FOUND" TO BRANCH-NAME.
```

Figure 3-7   Always reuse old code in new programs

Code each module with the goal of independence

Figure 3-8 presents the next critical principle. If you code each module so it's as independent as possible, you should be able to read the code without referring to other paragraphs in the program. This in turn makes it easier to read, test, and debug the program.

Of course, most modules are somewhat dependent on the processing done by other modules. If, for example, one module tests the value of a switch set by another module, the first module depends on the processing done by the second module. As a result, you can't code each module so it's completely independent of all other modules. In practice, you just do the best you can to keep each module as independent as possible.

One common way that programmers reduce module independence is illustrated in the example in figure 3-8. Here, modules 330 and 340 contain the control code that decides whether or not they do their own function. But this makes it impossible to read and understand module 320 without looking at the code in modules 330 and 340. To solve this problem, the IF logic in these modules should be moved up into module 320. Although that will make the code in module 320 somewhat harder to understand, you'll be able to read it without checking the code in other modules. In addition, the code for modules 330 and 340 will be simplified.

Similarly, to maintain module independence, you need to control the use of switches. In general, a switch should be turned on or off in a lower-level module and tested by modules that are higher up the leg. This can be described as *passing a switch* up the leg of a chart. In contrast, when you pass a switch down a leg or from one leg to another, it usually means that neither calling module nor called module are as independent as they could be.

Guidelines

- If a module is independent, you should be able to code and read the module without checking the code in other paragraphs.

- A module should *not* contain the control code that decides whether the function of the module is done. This reduces the independence of both the module and its calling module.

- Switches should be passed up the legs of a chart, not down or across.

Three modules that aren't independent because the second and third modules contain the control code that determines whether or not their own functions are done

```
 320-PRINT-CUSTOMER-LINE.
*
     PERFORM 330-SEARCH-BRANCH-TABLE.
     IF CM-BRANCH-NUMBER > OLD-BRANCH-NUMBER
         MOVE CM-BRANCH-NUMBER TO CL-BRANCH-NUMBER
         MOVE BRANCH-NAME TO CL-BRANCH-NAME
     ELSE
         MOVE SPACE TO CL-BRANCH-NAME
                       CL-BRANCH-NUMBER.
     PERFORM 340-PRINT-HEADING-LINES.
         .
         .
*
 330-SEARCH-BRANCH-TABLE.
*
     IF CM-BRANCH-NUMBER > OLD-BRANCH-NUMBER
         SET BT-INDEX TO 1
         SEARCH BT-ENTRIES
             AT END
                 MOVE "BRANCH NOT FOUND" TO BRANCH-NAME
             WHEN BT-BRANCH-NUMBER (BT-INDEX) = CM-BRANCH-NUMBER
                 MOVE BT-BRANCH-NAME (BT-INDEX) TO BRANCH-NAME
             WHEN BT-INDEX > BT-ENTRY-COUNT
                 MOVE "BRANCH NOT FOUND" TO BRANCH-NAME.
*
 340-PRINT-HEADING-LINES.
*
     IF LINE-COUNT > LINES-ON-PAGE
         ADD 1               TO PAGE-COUNT
         MOVE PAGE-COUNT     TO HDG1-PAGE-NUMBER
         MOVE HEADING-LINE-1 TO PRINT-AREA
         PERFORM 350-WRITE-PAGE-TOP-LINE
         MOVE HEADING-LINE-2 TO PRINT-AREA
         MOVE 1              TO SPACE-CONTROL
         PERFORM 360-WRITE-REPORT-LINE
         MOVE HEADING-LINE-3 TO PRINT-AREA
         PERFORM 360-WRITE-REPORT-LINE
         MOVE HEADING-LINE-4 TO PRINT-AREA
         MOVE 2              TO SPACE-CONTROL
         PERFORM 360-WRITE-REPORT-LINE
         MOVE 2              TO SPACE-CONTROL.
```

Figure 3-8   Code each module with the goal of independence

Code each module with the goal of clarity

Figure 3-9 presents the third critical principle. If the coding for a module is clear, it's easy to read, understand, and reuse in new programs. In addition to all of the coding guidelines presented thus far, this figure presents two more ideas for improving clarity.

First, don't use coding tricks that hide what a module does. This is illustrated by the first two examples in figure 3-9. The first example clearly shows the processing that's done for the first record that's read. The second example doesn't show that processing. For it to work, the OLD-BRANCH-NUMBER field must be set to blanks or LOW-VALUES in working storage (or by some earlier module). In this simple example, the coding differences aren't profound, but coding tricks are all too common in many production programs.

Second, when the coding in a module becomes cumbersome, you can move the code for trivial subfunctions like counting records and accumulating totals into the lowest-level modules in which those subfunctions are logical. This simplifies the code in the higher-level modules. This works particularly well if you establish conventions about which subfunctions belong in which types of modules. In our shop, for example, we agree that counting records belongs in the related Read or Write module.

Guidelines

- If a module is clear, you can read the module without checking the code in other modules and with minimal checking of the code in the Data Division. To make this work, you have to use meaningful data names in the Data Division.

- The code for a module should show what happens under what conditions. Don't use coding tricks that hide what a module does.

- To improve the clarity of a module, you can move subfunctions like counting records, accumulating totals, or performing calculations as far down that module's leg as possible. Or, you can move related subfunctions to a separate module that is called by a single PERFORM statement. These adjustments also make the subfunctions easier to find.

A print module that is coded with the goal of clarity

```
320-PRINT-CUSTOMER-LINE.
*
    IF FIRST-RECORD
        MOVE CM-BRANCH-NUMBER TO CL-BRANCH-NUMBER
        PERFORM 330-SEARCH-BRANCH-TABLE
        MOVE BRANCH-NAME TO CL-BRANCH-NAME
    ELSE
        IF CM-BRANCH-NUMBER > OLD-BRANCH-NUMBER
            MOVE CM-BRANCH-NUMBER TO CL-BRANCH-NUMBER
            PERFORM 330-SEARCH-BRANCH-TABLE
            MOVE BRANCH-NAME TO CL-BRANCH-NAME
        ELSE
            MOVE SPACE TO CL-BRANCH-NAME
                          CL-BRANCH-NUMBER.
    .
    .
```

The print module above when coded with fewer statements but less clarity

```
320-PRINT-CUSTOMER-LINE.
*
    IF CM-BRANCH-NUMBER > OLD-BRANCH-NUMBER
        MOVE CM-BRANCH-NUMBER TO CL-BRANCH-NUMBER
        PERFORM 330-SEARCH-BRANCH-TABLE
        MOVE BRANCH-NAME TO CL-BRANCH-NAME
    ELSE
        MOVE SPACE TO CL-BRANCH-NAME
                      CL-BRANCH-NUMBER.
    .
    .
```

A read module that includes a counting subfunction

```
310-READ-CUSTOMER-RECORD.
*
    READ CUSTMAST
        AT END
            MOVE "Y" TO CUSTMAST-EOF-SWITCH.
    IF NOT CUSTMAST-EOF
        ADD 1 TO MASTER-RECORD-COUNT.
```

Figure 3-9   Code each module with the goal of clarity

Perspective

To get the most from structured programming, it's not enough to use only the valid structures and to avoid the use of GO TO statements. You also need to follow coding conventions that make your programs easy to read and understand. And you need to code each module with independence and clarity as your goals.

If you do all that, your programs will be easy to debug and maintain. In addition, you'll be able to reuse large portions of the code in your old programs in new programs. And that's how you get the huge productivity gains that structured programming has always promised but rarely delivered.

Summary

- In COBOL, the PERFORM UNTIL and the IF statement are used for the iteration and selection structures.

- COBOL also provides for a *case structure* that can be implemented by nested IF statements or the EVALUATE statement that's part of the 1985 COBOL standards.

- *Structured delimiters* and *in-line PERFORM statements* can occasionally simplify the coding of a module. Both are part of the 1985 COBOL standards.

- *Coding conventions* are the rules and guidelines that are recommended in a COBOL shop. If all the programmers in the shop adhere to these conventions, the resulting programs will be easier to maintain.

- Some useful conventions in the Data Division are to group related data items (no 77 levels), to use consistent entry sequences in working storage, to use condition names for switch and code settings, and above all to use meaningful data names.

- Some useful conventions in the Procedure Division are to use only the valid structures (no GOTOs), to implement each module of a chart as a single COBOL paragraph, to keep the paragraphs in sequence by module number, and to use condition names.

- Three critical coding principles are: (1) always reuse old code in new programs; (2) code each module with the goal of independence; and (3) code each module with the goal of clarity.

Chapter 4

Top-down testing

When you design a structured program so it consists of independent, functional modules, you don't have to code the entire program before you start testing it. Instead, you can code and test a few modules at a time. This can help you make dramatic reductions in the time that it takes you to test a program. It can also help you improve the reliability of your programs.

An introduction to top-down testing

When you develop an unstructured program, you normally code the entire program before you start testing it. Then, you start testing the entire program. But if the program is lengthy, it is likely to contain dozens of bugs. For each one, whether it is trivial or complex, you have to find the error, correct it, recompile the entire program, and test the entire program again. This is likely to take dozens of test runs, and the entire process is likely to take longer than the time for design and coding combined.

In contrast, when you use *top-down testing* (which can also be called *top-down coding and testing*), you start by coding and testing the top module of the program plus a few subordinate modules. This is illustrated by phase 1 in figure 4-1. In this phase, only the unshaded modules are tested, and the shaded modules can be referred to as *program stubs*. The stubs are the modules that are called but aren't tested. As a result, they contain minimal code or no code at all.

Once the modules in phase 1 work correctly, you code and test a few more modules. This is illustrated by phase 2 in figure 4-1. When these modules plus the earlier modules work correctly, you continue with the next phase, and you continue this process until all of the modules have been coded and tested.

The benefits of top-down testing

When you use top-down coding and testing, you test a few dozen new statements at a time. As a result, it's relatively easy to locate the sources of any bugs because they are usually in the statements that you just added to the test run or in the interfaces between the new modules and the old ones. In addition, you test the program from the major control modules on down so you find the most critical errors first. Since this reduces testing time, it increases your productivity.

When you test only a few modules at a time, you can also make sure that each module is thoroughly tested. In contrast, when you test a large program all at once, you often find out much later that a few modules still contain bugs because you never tested them in the first place. That's why top-down testing is likely to reduce or eliminate the number of bugs that a program contains when it's put into production. In other words, top-down testing helps improve the reliability of your programs.

Those, of course, are the benefits that management appreciates: improved productivity and improved program reliability. But top-down testing also makes programming more satisfying for the programmer. Instead of coding for days at a time and then testing for more days at a time, top-down testing changes the nature of the job. Code and test a few modules, then code and test a few more, and before you know it another program is finished. Even better, you finish with the knowledge that you've tested every module and that every module works.

Phase 1

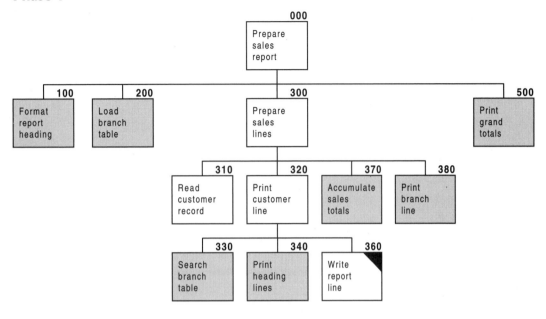

Phase 2

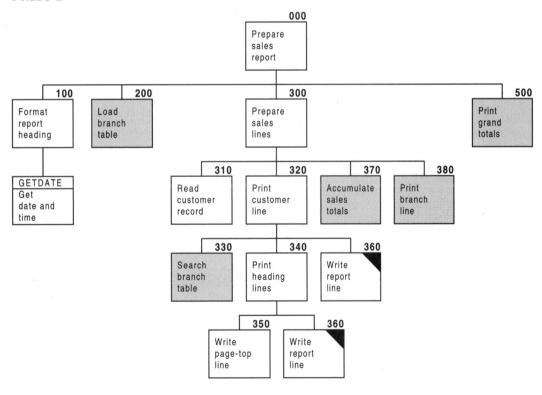

Note

- The shaded modules aren't tested. They are called *program stubs*.

Figure 4-1   Two phases of top-down testing for the report preparation program

The skills you need for top-down testing

To take advantage of top-down testing, you need just a few new skills. First, you need to know how to plan the coding and testing of a program. Second, you need to know how to code the modules that are going to be tested. Third, you need to know how to code the program stubs.

How to plan the sequence of coding and testing

Figure 4-2 presents a simple form that you can use for planning the test runs for a program. It also presents some guidelines for preparing the *test plan*. To show that there isn't just one right sequence for testing the modules, this figure presents two testing sequences that are both acceptable.

In the first test sequence in figure 4-2, the first two phases correspond to the charts in figure 4-1. In phase 1, the input data consists of just three records, and only customer lines are printed on the report. In phase 2, the modules for printing the heading lines are added. And in phase 3, the modules for printing the branch lines are added. These three phases test the critical logic of the program. After that, the modules for loading and searching the branch table and the module for printing grand totals are added.

In contrast, the second test sequence in figure 4-2 tests the critical logic of the program in the first two phases and doesn't even use test data until phase 3. Then, phase 3 can determine whether there are any bugs related to the data (a common problem). Phase 4 can determine whether there are any bugs related to the use of the subprogram (another common problem). And phase 5 can determine whether there are any bugs related to loading or searching the branch table (yet another common problem).

Which sequence of testing is better? That depends on the programmer. Yes, you should try to test the critical modules early in the plan. Otherwise, you can use the testing sequence that suits you best. Just be sure to take the time to make a plan.

Guidelines for preparing a test plan

- Test just a few modules at a time, but test all of the processing in each module.
- Test the critical modules of the program early in the plan.
- Test the remaining modules in whatever sequence you prefer.
- Keep the test data to a minimum in the early test phases.

A top-down test plan for the report preparation program

Program name	MKTG1200	**Page**	1
Program description	Prepare Sales Report	**Date**	11/20/96

The sequence of modules to be tested

Phase	Modules	Test data
1	000, 300, 310, 320, and 360	Three customer records: 2 for one branch and 1 for a second branch
2	Add 100, 340, and 350	Same as above
3	Add 370 and 380	Same as above
4	Add 200, 210, and 330	Two table records with one for the first branch number used in the three customer records, but none for the second branch number
5	Add 500	Same as above
6	All modules	Enough customer records to test page overflow

Another acceptable sequence of modules to be tested

Phase	Modules	Test data
1	000, 300, 320, 340, 350, and 360	Simulate one input record in the program stub for module 310
2	Add 370 and 380	Same as above
3	Add 310	Three customer records: 2 for one branch and 1 for a second branch
4	Add 100 and 500	Same as above
5	Add 200, 210, and 330	Two table records with one for the first branch number used in the three customer records, but none for the second branch number
6	All modules	Enough customer records to test page overflow

Figure 4-2   How to prepare a test plan for top-down testing

How to code the new modules for each phase of testing

Figure 4-3 presents some basic guidelines for coding the new modules for each phase of testing. Notice that you don't have to code the complete Environment or Data Division before you start testing the program. Instead, you only need to code the entries that are required by the Procedure Division modules that are going to be tested.

In phase 1 of the first sequence in figure 4-2, for example, only customer lines are going to be printed. As a result, you don't have to code the Data Division entries for the heading, branch, or total lines before this test run. Instead, you can add these entries when you test the modules that print the heading, branch, and total lines. Similarly, you don't have to include the Environment Division entries for the branch master file in the code for phase 1 because it isn't required until phase 4.

In general, you should code each Procedure Division module in its entirety when you add it to the program. Then, if you want to exclude the processing for one or more lines in a specific test run, you can add an asterisk to column 7 of the line so it's treated as a comment. Later on, when you're ready for that line to be executed, you can remove the asterisk.

In the first example in figure 4-3, you can see how asterisks in column 7 are used to treat portions of the OPEN and CLOSE statements in the top-level module as comments. Later, when modules 200 and 210 are added to the program, the asterisks can be removed.

In the second example in figure 4-3, asterisks are used to treat the PERFORM statements for modules 370 and 380 as comments. If you comment out the last line in a nested IF, though, you have to add a period at an appropriate point earlier in the nest. That can cause problems when you remove the comments later on. The alternative is to enter just the paragraph names for these modules into the Procedure Division so these modules can be performed without doing any processing.

Guidelines

- To start, code the Identification Division and as much of the Environment and Data Divisions as are needed for the phase 1 testing. Then, code the Procedure Division modules that are going to be tested.

- When you add new modules for the next phase of testing, code the new modules in the Procedure Division as well as any required code in the Environment or Data Division.

- If necessary, put an asterisk (*) in column 7 of any Procedure Division statement that you don't want executed during a test run. (If you comment out the last line in a series of nested IFs, though, you may have to make other adjustments too as shown in the second example below.)

How parts of an OPEN statement can be treated as comments

```
 PROCEDURE DIVISION.
*
 000-PREPARE-SALES-REPORT.
*
     OPEN INPUT   CUSTMAST
*                 BRCHMAST
           OUTPUT SALESRPT.
     PERFORM 100-FORMAT-REPORT-HEADING.
     PERFORM 200-LOAD-BRANCH-TABLE.
     PERFORM 300-PREPARE-SALES-LINES
         UNTIL CUSTMAST-EOF.
     PERFORM 500-PRINT-GRAND-TOTALS.
     CLOSE CUSTMAST
*           BRCHMAST
           SALESRPT.
     STOP RUN.
```

How PERFORM statements can be treated as comments

```
 300-PREPARE-SALES-LINES.
*
     PERFORM 310-READ-CUSTOMER-RECORD.
     IF NOT CUSTMAST-EOF
         IF FIRST-RECORD
             MOVE CM-BRANCH-NUMBER TO OLD-BRANCH-NUMBER
             PERFORM 320-PRINT-CUSTOMER-LINE
*            PERFORM 370-ACCUMULATE-SALES-TOTALS
             MOVE  N  TO FIRST-RECORD-SWITCH
         ELSE
             IF CM-BRANCH-NUMBER = OLD-BRANCH-NUMBER
                 PERFORM 320-PRINT-CUSTOMER-LINE
*                PERFORM 370-ACCUMULATE-SALES-TOTALS
             ELSE
*                PERFORM 380-PRINT-BRANCH-LINE
                 PERFORM 320-PRINT-CUSTOMER-LINE
*                PERFORM 370-ACCUMULATE-SALES-TOTALS
                 MOVE CM-BRANCH-NUMBER TO OLD-BRANCH-NUMBER.
*    ELSE
*        PERFORM 380-PRINT-BRANCH-LINE.
```

Figure 4-3   How to code the new modules to be tested

75

How to code the program stubs

Figure 4-4 presents the guidelines for coding the program stubs that are required for a test run. These are the modules that are called by other modules, but are not actually part of the test run.

If a program stub doesn't have to do anything for the test run to work properly, the stub can consist of just the paragraph name. This is illustrated by the first example in figure 4-4. Then, when the paragraph is performed, nothing is done and the program continues.

A step above this is to include a DISPLAY statement in the stub that displays the name of the module on the screen to show that it has been executed. This is illustrated by the second example in figure 4-4.

For a program stub that represents an input module, it sometimes make sense to simulate the reading of one or more records in the file. If, for example, the test data for a program isn't ready yet, this lets you start testing the program without waiting for the data. In the third example in figure 4-4, the read stub just indicates that all the records in the file have been read. In the fourth example, the read stub simulates the reading of one record the first time it's executed and indicates that all the records in the file have been read the second time it's executed.

Similarly, a table-loading stub can simulate the loading of a few records of the table. A search stub can simulate the search of a table. And an output stub can display a record on the screen instead of writing the record on a file or printing it. These options are illustrated by the last three examples in figure 4-4.

As you create your program stubs, the goal is to get the testing done right with a minimum of extra work. In most cases, you can do that with simple stubs that cause little extra work, but improve the results that you get from top-down testing. When a program stub starts getting too elaborate, you're usually better off coding the entire module and adding it to that test phase.

Guidelines

- If a program stub doesn't have to do anything for the successful completion of a test run, the module can consist of the paragraph name only.
- If you want to see whether a program stub gets executed during a test run, you can include a statement that displays the module name.
- If necessary, an input stub can simulate the reading of one or more records; a table-loading stub can simulate the loading of one or more entry sets; a search stub can simulate the searching of a table; and so on.

A processing stub that consists of only the paragraph name

```
 370-ACCUMULATE-SALES-TOTALS.
*
```

A processing stub that displays its module name

```
 370-ACCUMULATE-SALES-TOTALS.
*
     DISPLAY "370-ACCUMULATE-SALES-TOTALS".
```

An input stub that displays its module name and sets a switch

```
 310-READ-CUSTOMER-RECORD.
*
     DISPLAY "310-READ-CUSTOMER-RECORD".
     MOVE "Y" TO CUSTMAST-EOF-SWITCH.
```

An input stub that simulates the reading of one input record, then sets the end-of-file switch

```
 310-READ-CUSTOMER-RECORD.
*
     IF FIRST-RECORD
         MOVE "0199123450RIGINAL SYSTEMS, INC."
             TO CUSTOMER-MASTER-RECORD
     ELSE
         MOVE "Y" TO CUSTMAST-EOF-SWITCH.
```

A table-loading stub that simulates the loading of two sets of entries

```
 200-LOAD-BRANCH-TABLE.
*
     MOVE "01INDIANAPOLIS" TO BT-ENTRIES (1).
     MOVE "02CLEVELAND"    TO BT-ENTRIES (2).
     MOVE "Y" TO BRCHMAST-EOF-SWITCH.
```

A search stub that sets the switch that indicates the search argument can't be found

```
 330-SEARCH-BRANCH-TABLE.
*
     MOVE "N" TO BRANCH-FOUND-SWITCH.
```

An output stub that displays a record instead of writing it

```
 400-WRITE-MASTER-RECORD.
*
     DISPLAY "400-WRITE-MASTER-RECORD".
     DISPLAY CUSTOMER-MASTER-RECORD.
```

Figure 4-4   How to code program stubs

Perspective

When you design and code your programs using the structured techniques of chapters 2 and 3, you can also use top-down testing. It provides another way to increase productivity and improve program quality. In fact, the benefits that you get from this type of testing are often dramatic.

To take advantage of top-down testing requires just a few simple skills. It is valuable for programs as short as a few hundred lines. And the larger a program is, the more valuable this technique becomes. Shouldn't you try it on your next program?

Summary

- When you use *top-down coding and testing* (or just *top-down testing*), you code and test a few modules of the program at a time. This makes the testing process more manageable, reduces the time that it takes to test a program, and improves the reliability of the program (fewer bugs).

- When you plan the testing of a structured program, you create a *test plan* that shows the sequence that the modules of the program will be tested in. The test plan can also describe the test data that will be used in each phase of testing.

- As you add new modules to the program, you code the Procedure Division paragraphs as well as any new entries that are required in the Environment or Data Division.

- A *program stub* is a module that is called during a test run but not tested. The code for a program stub can range from just the paragraph name for the module to code that simulates the processing that must be done by the module.

Chapter 5

Structured design and coding for interactive programs

In chapters 2, 3, and 4, a simple *batch* program was used to illustrate the principles of structured design, structured coding, and top-down testing. Those principles, however, can be applied to all types of programs, large and small, including both batch and interactive programs.

In this chapter, you'll learn how to apply those principles to interactive programs. First, you'll learn how to design interactive programs for midrange computers or PC networks using COBOL compilers like Micro Focus COBOL or Ryan McFarland COBOL. Then, you'll learn the special design and coding requirements for interactive CICS programs written for mainframe computers. When you finish this chapter, you'll have a better understanding of how the principles of chapters 2, 3, and 4 can be applied to all types of COBOL programs.

The specifications and planning for an interactive program

Before you start the design of an interactive program, you often need to do some extra planning that isn't required by batch programs. In particular, you need to decide what screens are going to be used by the program and what keys will be used to start actions from each of the screens.

The program specifications for an interactive program

Figure 5-1 presents the specifications for a simple interactive program that is used to maintain the records in a file of customer master records. It requires the use of two different *screens* that are displayed on the computer user's monitor (or *terminal* on a mainframe system). The first screen is a customer key screen; the second one is a customer data screen.

When the program starts, the key screen is displayed. At this screen, the user enters a customer key and an action code that tells whether the user wants to add, change, or delete the record with that customer key. If the combination of key and action code is valid, the program displays the data screen so the user can complete the action. Then, after an action has been completed, the program displays the key screen again so the user can add, change, or delete another record. At either screen, if the computer user presses the F3 key, the program ends.

As simple as this program is, its design and coding illustrates how the principles of structured programming can be applied to all interactive programs. For instance, all interactive programs must *accept* the data that is entered into the keyboard of a workstation or terminal. This can be referred to as "accepting the data from a screen" because the data appears on the screen as the user types it. In most cases, the data that's accepted must then be *edited*. This means that the data must be checked for validity before it is used for processing. Modules for purposes like these are clearly illustrated by this simple program.

Program specifications

Program name	CUSTMNT1	Page	1
Program description	Maintain customer file	Date	11/20/96

Input/output specifications

File name	Description	Format	Use
CUSTMAST	Customer master file	Indexed	I-O
SCREEN1	Customer key screen	Screen	I-O
SCREEN2	Customer data screen	Screen	I-O

Processing specifications

- When the key screen is displayed, the user enters a customer key and an action code. If the user selects Add, the customer key must not be in the master file. If the user selects Change or Delete, the customer key must be in the master file.

- If the user enters a valid combination of customer key and action, the program displays the data screen. For an Add, the user enters the new customer information on this screen. For a Change, the user modifies one or more of the fields that are displayed. For a Deletion, the user confirms that this is the record that should be deleted.

- If the user presses F3 at either the key screen or the maintenance screen, the program should end and return to the menu program that started it.

- If the user presses F12 from the key screen, the program should also end and return to the menu program that started it. However, if the user presses F12 from the data screen, the program should return to the key screen without processing any of the data that was entered.

The screen layouts for the program

Figure 5-2 presents the two screen layouts for this program. The first one is for the key screen. The second one is for the customer data screen. The rows of X's in lines 3 and 23 of these screens indicate that messages can be moved into these areas before the screens are displayed. In line 24 of each screen, you can see a message that says you can exit from the program by pressing the F3 key and you can cancel the current action by pressing the F12 key.

When you develop an interactive program, you may be responsible for the design of the screens. You may also be responsible for identifying the special keys that are going to be used to initiate actions from each screen, like the F3 and F12 keys on most keyboards or like the PF3, PF12, or Clear key on a CICS terminal. In most COBOL shops, standards are available for the layouts of screens including the use of message lines and special keys. This consistency from one program to the next makes it easier for the computer users to use the programs.

But even if layout standards are available, you usually have to make some decisions of your own. Sometimes, you may decide that other special keys need to be used. Sometimes, you may decide that other screens are needed. To simplify the design and coding of a complicated maintenance program, for example, you could have one screen for adding records, one for changing them, and one for verifying deletions.

The layout for the key screen

```
Customer Maintenance

Type a customer number.  Then select an action and press Enter.

Customer number. . . . . XXXXXX

Action . . . . . . . . . X 1.  Add a new customer
                           2.  Change an existing customer
                           3.  Delete an existing customer




















XXXXXXXXXXXXXXXXXXXXXXXXXXXXXXXXXXXXXXXXXXXXXXXXXXXXXXXXXXXXXXXXXXXXXXXXX:
F3=Exit    F12=Cancel
```

The layout for the customer data screen

```
Customer Maintenance

XXXXXXXXXXXXXXXXXXXXXXXXXXXXXXXXXXXXXXXXXXXXXXXXXXXXXXXXXXXXXXXXXXXXXXXXXX

Customer number. . . . . XXXXXX

Last name. . . . . . . . XXXXXXXXXXXXXXXXXXXXXXXXXXXXXXX
First name . . . . . . . XXXXXXXXXXXXXXXXXXX
Address. . . . . . . . . XXXXXXXXXXXXXXXXXXXXXXXXXXXXXX
City . . . . . . . . . . XXXXXXXXXXXXXXXXXXX
State. . . . . . . . . . XX
Zip code . . . . . . . . XXXXXXXXX











XXXXXXXXXXXXXXXXXXXXXXXXXXXXXXXXXXXXXXXXXXXXXXXXXXXXXXXXXXXXXXXXXXXXXXXXXX
F3=Exit    F12=Cancel
```

Figure 5-2   The screen layouts for the interactive program

An event/response chart for the program

An *event* in interactive terms is a user action like pressing the Enter key that sends the screen entries to the program. The *response* is the processing that the program does for that event. Because one screen layout can be the source of many events, it often helps to summarize the events and responses before starting the design of an interactive program.

Figure 5-3 presents a form that can be used to summarize the events and responses of a program. To start, you can summarize the *contexts* of the program. At the least, there should be one context for each screen of the program. However, there can be more than one context for each screen. In this figure, for example, three contexts have been identified for the customer data screen because the responses vary depending on whether the customer data screen is used for an addition, a change, or a deletion.

Once you understand the contexts, you can complete the second portion of this form by listing the response to each event in each context. It also helps to identify the new context for each response. When you're done, you should have a clear idea of what your program needs to provide for.

Keep in mind, though, that a form like the one in figure 5-3 is just a working paper that you can use as a planning tool for the design and coding of a program. As a result, you can use whatever notation you prefer in this form because you won't keep the form as part of the program's documentation. Also, as you gain experience with interactive programs, you'll be able to reduce the amount of detail that you record on this form.

Event/response chart

Program name	CUSTMNT1	Page	1
Program description	Maintain customer file	Date	11/20/96

Context summary

Context	Description
Get key	The key screen is displayed.
Add customer	The data screen is displayed after a request to add a customer.
Change customer	The data screen is displayed after a request to change a customer.
Delete customer	The data screen is displayed after a request to delete a customer.

Event/response summary

Event	Context	Response	New context
Start	N/A	Display the key screen.	Get key
F3	All	Return to calling program.	N/A
F12	Get key	Return to calling program.	N/A
	Add customer Change customer Delete customer	Cancel operation and display the key screen.	Get key
Enter	Get key	Edit the input data. If valid 　　display the data screen Else 　　display an error message.	 Add customer, Change customer, or Delete customer Get key
	Add customer	Edit the input data. If valid 　　add the customer record 　　display the key screen Else 　　display an error message.	 Get key Add customer
	Change customer	Edit the input data. If valid 　　change customer record 　　display the key screen Else 　　display an error message.	 Get key Change customer
	Delete customer	Delete the customer record. Display the key screen.	 Get key
Other key	All	Display an error message.	Unchanged

Figure 5-3　An event/response chart for the interactive program

How to design an interactive program

Once you've planned the screen layouts, events, and responses for a program, you can design the program using a structure chart just as you design a batch program. To some extent, though, your thinking changes when you design an interactive program. Instead of focusing on what the program is going to do, you must focus on how the program is going to handle the major events of the program. This can be referred as *event-driven processing*.

How to design the top levels

Figure 5-4 shows how to design the top levels of an interactive program. Just as you do with a batch program, the top module represents the entire program, and it repeatedly executes one primary module at the next level. To indicate the event-driven nature of this program, the top module in this example is named "Process customer trans" (which is short for "Process customer transactions") and the primary module at the next level is named "Process customer transaction." (At these levels, names like "Maintain customer file" and "Maintain customer record" work just as well, but you may as well get into the event-driven state of mind).

At the third level of the program, you usually create one module for each context of the program. Here again, to indicate the event-driven nature of the program, names like "Process customer addition" and "Process customer change" are used. These names indicate that there is more to these modules than just adding or changing a record. That's why names like "Add customer record" or "Change customer record" aren't as appropriate.

Another approach to the design of the third level is to create one module for each of the major responses to events. In general, if a response receives data from a screen, processes it, and returns data to screen, a separate module should be created for it. If you refer back to figure 5-3, you can see that the only responses that do that are the responses when the Enter key is pressed in each of the four contexts of the program. So this approach also leads to the design in figure 5-4. All of the other responses are so trivial that they don't require separate modules.

When you use some compilers, you need to add one module at the second level that gets the program ready to display and accept the screens. In figure 5-4, this module is named "Enable screen handling." You can see how this works with the Micro Focus compiler in model program 3.

The top three levels of the interactive program

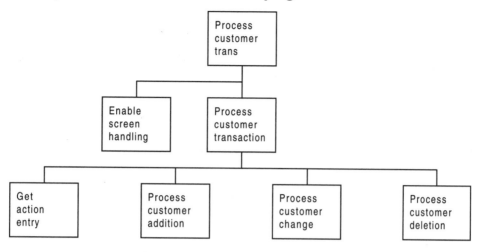

A general procedure for designing the top three levels

1. Draw the top module and give it a name that represents the entire program. If possible, the name should reflect the event-driven nature of the program.

2. Draw the primary control module at the second level that's subordinate to the top module, and give it a name that reflects event-driven processing.

3. Draw any modules at the second level that have to be done before or after the primary module. This is likely to include a module that prepares a program for screen handling as indicated by the enable-screen-handling module shown above.

4. Draw the modules at the third level that are required by the primary control module in the second level. Usually, there should be one module for each context of the program or one module for each of the major responses of the program. You can usually determine this by studying the event/response chart for a program. Here again, use module names that reflect event-driven processing.

Figure 5-4   How to design the first three levels of an interactive program

How to design the legs

Figure 5-5 shows two of the legs of the interactive maintenance program. To design them, you use the same principles that you use for designing the legs of a batch program. Just divide each module into its component functions and make sure that each subordinate module is functionally subordinate to the module that calls it.

For a module that gets data like the get-action-entry and get-customer-data modules in this figure, you usually design at least two subordinate modules. One of these modules accepts the data from the screen like the accept-action-screen module. The other module is an edit module that checks the user entries for validity. In some cases, you may include a verify module that gives the user a chance to verify that the edited data and the intended action are in fact correct, but that goes back to the event/response planning that you do.

The legs in this figure assume that you're using a compiler that accepts all the data entered into a screen by executing just one statement (usually, an ACCEPT statement). Then, each edit module edits all the fields that have been accepted from the screen. This is the way the compilers for most business systems work.

Some PC compilers, though, can accept only one field of data at a time. In that case, the design of the legs may be changed significantly because you may need to have one "Get field" module for each field that's accepted from a screen. Subordinate to the get-action-entry module, for example, you would have one module for getting the customer key and another one for getting the action code. Then, subordinate to each of these modules, you would have an accept module and an edit module. This, of course, adds many modules to a structure chart. It isn't illustrated in this book, however, because this type of programming usually isn't used for business programs.

The get-action-entry leg

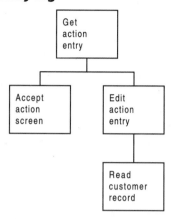

The process-customer-addition leg

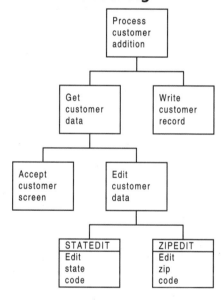

A general procedure for designing one leg of an interactive program

1. Draw one module for each function that the control level module at the top of the leg needs to do. For a module that gets entries from a screen, this usually includes one module for accepting the data and another module for editing the data. This is shown by the two subordinates for the get-action-entry module.

2. Continue this process until each of the lowest-level modules consists of just one function. Here again, a module that gets entries from a screen usually has at least one subordinate module for accepting the entries and another one for editing the entries.

Figure 5-5   How to design the legs of an interactive program

How to complete the structure chart

Figure 5-6 shows the complete structure chart for the interactive maintenance program. Like a structure chart for a batch program, you need to add the Read, Write, and Rewrite modules that isolate the READ, WRITE, and REWRITE statements for a program. In addition, for an interactive program, it usually makes sense to isolate the statements that accept data from screens in their own modules. In this example, that just means that module 420 is added as a subordinate to module 610.

Once you've got all the modules on the chart, you just mark the common modules and number all of the modules. The end result is a program design that's based on the same principles that batch program design is based on. The primary difference is that the names and structure reflect the requirements of event-driven processing.

The complete structure chart

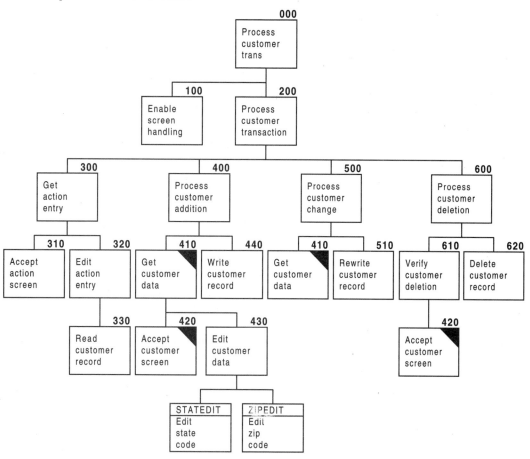

A general procedure for completing a structure chart

1. If necessary, add one Read, Write, or Rewrite module for each READ, WRITE, or REWRITE statement required by disk and print operations.

2. If necessary, add one Accept module for each screen that's used by the program. That way, the module can be called from the other legs of the chart whenever it's needed.

3. Shade the corners of the common modules.

4. Number the modules in the program.

Design differences for CICS programs

When you develop interactive COBOL programs on a mainframe computer, you usually use CICS (Customer Information Control System) for the interactive portions of the processing. Since CICS has requirements that go beyond those of COBOL, this forces some design changes that aren't found in other types of COBOL programs. Most of these changes are based on the requirement for pseudo-conversational processing.

The rest of this chapter presents the design and coding differences for CICS programs. It assumes that you already know how to develop CICS programs, so the emphasis is on how you can improve your design and coding methods. For those of you who aren't already familiar with CICS, these topics can serve as an introduction to CICS.

How pseudo-conversational processing works

Figure 5-7 presents the differences between *conversational processing*, which is the norm for interactive processing, and *pseudo-conversational processing,* which is used with CICS. When you use conversational processing, the computer displays a screen of information on the computer user's terminal, the user responds with keyboard input that gets sent back to the computer, the computer sends another screen of information, and so on. While the computer waits for a response from the computer user, the program remains active even though it's idle.

That works okay if the program handles a limited number of interactive users, but a CICS system on a mainframe computer usually handles hundreds of users. As a result, processing efficiency is far more important on a CICS system than it is on smaller systems. And holding system resources idle while a program waits for user responses is unacceptable.

To eliminate this waiting time, pseudo-conversational processing is used. That means that a program ends each time it sends a screen of data to the computer terminal. This frees the system resources used by the program. Then, when the terminal user completes the input and sends the screen of data back to the computer system, the program is restarted. Because millions of computer operations can be done in a second, pseudo-conversational processing improves the overall efficiency of a CICS system even if the average user response takes just a few seconds.

The trouble with pseudo-conversational processing is that it increases the complexity of an interactive program. This shows up in both the design and coding of the program.

**Conversational
processing**

**Pseudo-conversational
processing**

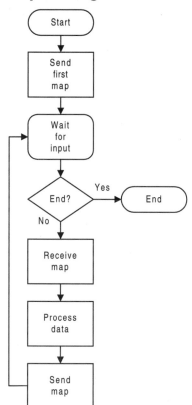

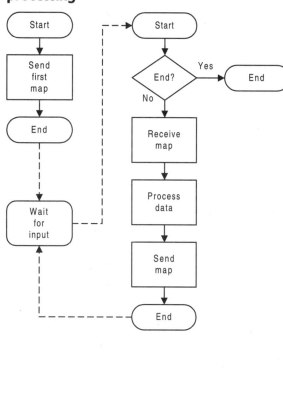

Notes

- With conversational processing, the program keeps running until the user is finished with the program and ends it. This is the way interactive programs work on most systems.

- With CICS on a mainframe, though, you use pseudo-conversational processing. Then, the program ends each time it sends a screen (map) to a terminal. This frees the program's resources while the CICS system waits for the terminal user to enter the required data.

- When the terminal user presses a key that sends the map back to the system, the program is restarted. Then, the program receives the map, processes the data, sends an appropriate map back to the user's terminal, and ends again.

- This process continues until the terminal user presses a key that indicates that the program should end.

Figure 5-7   How pseudo-conversational processing differs from conversational
processing

How to design the top levels of a CICS program

Figure 5-8 presents the design for the top two levels of a CICS program that has the specifications presented in figures 5-1, 5-2, and 5-3. If you compare these top levels with the top levels in figure 5-4, you can see that one level has been removed from the CICS chart. That's because each execution of the program does the processing for only one screen of information. As a result, there's no need for the top module to repeatedly call one primary module at the next level. In other words, the top module in figure 5-8 is equivalent to the primary module in the second level of figure 5-4.

To design the modules at the second level of the CICS chart, you use the same type of thinking that you use for the third level of a normal interactive program. In general, there should be one module for each of the major responses or contexts that you've planned.

If you're already familiar with CICS, you know that a screen is referred to as a *map* when you use CICS. When a program *sends* a map, the map is displayed on a terminal. When a program *receives* a map, the keyboard input is returned to the program. This terminology should of course be used in the names of modules that process, send, or receive maps.

The first two levels of a CICS program

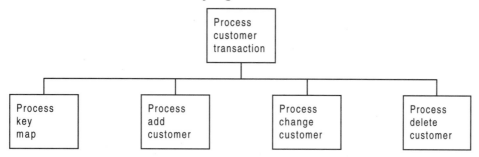

A general procedure for designing the first two levels

1. Draw the top module and give it a name that represents the processing for one screen of data. The name should reflect the event-driven nature of the program.

2. Draw the modules at the next level that are required by the top module. Usually, there should be one module for each context of the program or one module for each of the major responses of the program. You can usually determine this by studying the event/response chart for a program. Here again, use module names that reflect event-driven processing.

Note

- When you work with CICS, screens are referred to as *maps*. As a result, the word *map* should be used in place of the word *screen* in any module names.

Figure 5-8   How to design the first two levels of a CICS program

95

How to design the legs of a CICS program

Figure 5-9 presents a general procedure for designing the legs that do the processing for one map or the processing for one context of a map. In general, the top module in this type of leg usually calls (1) a module for receiving the data in the map, (2) a module for editing the data received from the map, and (3) one module for sending each map that's required back to the terminal. The top module may also call modules for functions like reading or writing records in files.

As you plan the modules for a map processing leg, you should refer back to the event/response chart. If you refer back to figure 5-3, for example, you can see that the leg for processing the key map sends either the data map or the key map back to the terminal and so do the legs for processing additions and changes. In contrast, the leg for processing deletions always sends the key map back to the terminal.

After you design the first level of subordinate modules in a leg, you of course continue the process. For instance, the edit module for the key map requires a subordinate module that reads the customer record for the key that has been entered. Similarly, the edit module for the customer map would at least require subprogram modules for editing the state code and zip code. To simplify this chart, however, these modules have been omitted.

In the process-change-customer leg of the program, please note that one of the modules reads a customer record "for update." This holds the customer record so no other program can change it before it is rewritten on the disk. This module is necessary because the customer record that's read when the key map is edited is released when the program sends the customer map to the terminal and the program ends.

But what happens if some other program changes the record between the time it is first read and the time it is read for update? Since this would lead to errors, the code in the process-change-customer module must provide for it (although this has no effect on the structure chart). You can see how this is handled in the code for module 3000 in model program 4.

The process-key-map leg

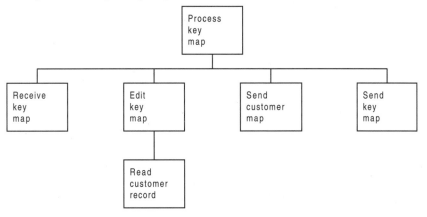

The process-add-customer leg

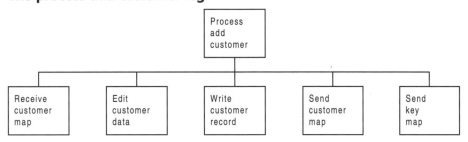

The process-change-customer leg

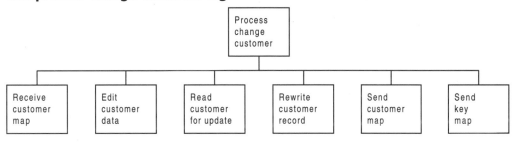

A general procedure for designing the map-processing legs

1. Draw one module for receiving the map.

2. Draw one module for editing the data that's received.

3. Draw one module for each map that may have to be sent back to the terminal.

4. Draw one module for any other functions that are required at this level. To add a customer to the master file, for example, the process-add-customer leg requires the write-customer-record module. To change a customer record, the process-change-customer leg requires the read-customer-for-update module and the rewrite-customer-record modules.

Figure 5-9   How to design the map-processing legs of a CICS program

97

How to complete the design of a CICS program

Figure 5-10 shows the complete chart for the interactive file maintenance program when you use CICS. Because so many modules are required just for sending and receiving maps, the structure chart for a CICS program is normally spread over several pages. Nevertheless, the simple design guidelines that this chapter presents should help you keep your modules manageable.

If you look at the process-delete-customer leg of this chart, you may be surprised to see that there aren't subordinate modules for receiving the customer map and editing the data in it. That's because the terminal user just presses the Enter key to confirm that a record should be deleted; no data is entered or received. Since this event can be handled by the top module of the program as shown in figure 5-12, receiving and editing modules aren't needed in this leg of the program.

Similarly, you may wonder why modules for sending the customer map and the key map have to be added to the second level of this chart as common modules. The answer is that one of these modules is called to send the screen back to the user whenever the user returns a screen to the program by pressing an invalid key. These modules are called from the top module because this module determines what event has occurred and what the response should be as shown in figure 5-12.

The complete structure chart for the CICS maintenance program

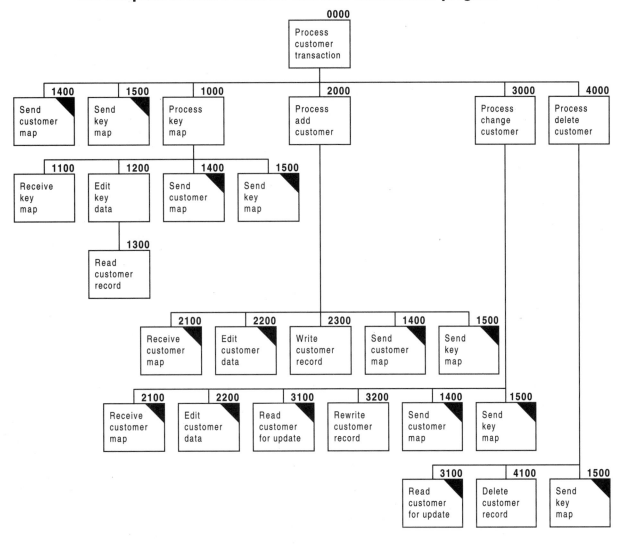

A general procedure for completing the structure chart

1. Add a common module to the second level for sending each of the maps that the program requires (like modules 1400 and 1500 above). These modules are called by the top module whenever a users sends a map back to the program by pressing an invalid key.

2. If necessary, add one I/O module for each READ, WRITE, REWRITE, or DELETE statement required by disk and print operations.

3. Shade the corners of the common modules, and number the modules in the program.

Figure 5-10   How to complete the structure chart for a CICS program   99

Coding conventions for CICS programs

The coding conventions that follow are designed to help you improve the structure of your CICS code. This is based on the assumption that you already know how to code a CICS program. If you have any difficulty following these conventions because you're not used to coding CICS programs this way, you may want to refer to our CICS book for more information (*CICS for the COBOL Programmmer, Part 1*).

Data Division conventions

Figure 5-11 gives a simple set of conventions for the Data Division along with some coding examples. Just as you do with batch programs, you should code the entries in a consistent sequence from one program to another and use indentation and blank comment lines to make the code easier to read. Beyond that, this figure gives specific recommendations for the use of a communication area, the DFHCOMMAREA in the Linkage Section, and a COPY member for the attributes that can be applied to the fields in a map.

Recommendations

- Use the same sequences of code in all your CICS programs.
- Code your own COPY member for attribute characters or use the one that's part of your shop standards because the one supplied by IBM is cumbersome. You can see the COPY member that we use in model program 4.
- Code a group of Working Storage fields named COMMUNICATION-AREA for the fields that you want to save when you send a screen to a terminal and end the program as part of the pseudo-conversational logic. An effective example is shown below.
- Code your own DFHCOMMAREA in the Linkage Section as shown below. This area should correspond to the COMMUNICATION-AREA in Working Storage. If you don't code your own area, the CICS translator defines a one-byte area automatically.

A recommended coding sequence

Communication area
    Switches and flags
    Control total fields
    Record descriptions
Symbolic maps (the COPY members generated by BMS)
A COPY member for attribute characters (your shop's or your own)
The IBM-supplied DFHAID COPY member
A COPY member for unrecoverable error parameters (if needed)
Linkage section
    DFHCOMMAREA

A communication area for the interactive maintenance program

```
01  COMMUNICATION-AREA.
*
    05  CA-CONTEXT-FLAG                 PIC X.
        88  PROCESS-KEY-MAP                         VALUE '1'.
        88  PROCESS-ADD-CUSTOMER                    VALUE '2'.
        88  PROCESS-CHANGE-CUSTOMER                 VALUE '3'.
        88  PROCESS-DELETE-CUSTOMER                 VALUE '4'.
    05  CA-CUSTOMER-RECORD.
        10  CA-CUSTOMER-NUMBER          PIC X(6).
        10  FILLER                      PIC X(112).
```

A Linkage Section that corresponds to the communication area

```
 LINKAGE SECTION.
*
 01  DFHCOMMAREA                        PIC X(119).
```

Figure 5-11   Data Division conventions for CICS programs

The top module in the Procedure Division

Figure 5-12 presents structured coding for the top module of the interactive maintenance program. Here, the EVALUATE statement is used to direct the processing. Within that statement, the first WHEN clause tests whether the communication area has a length of zero (EIBCALEN = ZERO). If it does, that means that the program has just started so the key map is sent to the terminal.

After that, the WHEN clauses direct the processing for specific *attention (or AID) keys*. These are the keys that the terminal user can press to send the map back to CICS. As a result, there's one WHEN clause for the PF3 key, one for the PF12 key, one for the Clear key, one for the Enter key, and one for the PA keys. Although this coding provides for more keys than are shown in the program specifications (figure 5-1) or the event/response chart (figure 5-3), this is often true for a CICS program. Because the specifications and the event/response chart emphasize the main processing functions, they don't necessarily list all of the possible error keys, even though the program has to provide for them.

In case you're not familiar with the EVALUATE statement, it became available with the VS COBOL II compiler. When it is executed, the statements after only one of the WHEN clauses are executed. Then, the processing continues with the first statement after the EVALUATE statement. Although you can get the same results by using IF statements, the EVALUATE statement makes this processing relatively easy to follow with a reduced chance for bugs.

Within the EVALUATE statement, you can see two CICS XCTL statements. These statements end the terminal session and start the CICS program named INVMENU. Appropriately, these statements are executed in the WHEN clause for the PF3 key and in the WHEN clause for the PF12 key (but only as part of the processing for the key map). After the EVALUATE statement, the CICS RETURN statement is used to end the program as part of the pseudo-conversational logic.

The coding in this figure also illustrates the use of the SET TO TRUE statement that became available with the VS COBOL II compiler. This statement is used to turn on the flags used by the program, which is easier to understand than moving a value to a flag. As a result, the use of this statement can improve the clarity of your code.

Source code for the first Procedure Division paragraph

```
0000-PROCESS-CUSTOMER-TRAN.
*
        MOVE DFHCOMMAREA TO COMMUNICATION-AREA.
        EVALUATE TRUE
            WHEN EIBCALEN = ZERO————————————————No communication area
                MOVE LOW-VALUE TO MNTMAP10
                MOVE -1 TO CUSTNO1L
                SET SEND-ERASE TO TRUE
                PERFORM 1500-SEND-KEY-MAP
                SET PROCESS-KEY-MAP TO TRUE
            WHEN EIBAID = DFHPF3————————————————————PF3 key
                EXEC CICS
                    XCTL PROGRAM('INVMENU')
                END-EXEC
            WHEN EIBAID = DFHPF12———————————————————PF12 key
                IF PROCESS-KEY-MAP
                    EXEC CICS
                        XCTL PROGRAM('INVMENU')
                    END-EXEC
                ELSE
                    MOVE LOW-VALUE TO MNTMAP10
                    MOVE -1 TO CUSTNO1L
                    SET SEND-ERASE TO TRUE
                    PERFORM 1500-SEND-KEY-MAP
                    SET PROCESS-KEY-MAP TO TRUE
            WHEN EIBAID = DFHCLEAR——————————————————Clear key
                .
                .
            WHEN EIBAID = DFHPA1 OR DFHPA2 OR DFHPA3————————PA key
                CONTINUE
            WHEN EIBAID = DFHENTER ——————————————————Enter key
                IF PROCESS-KEY-MAP
                    PERFORM 1000-PROCESS-KEY-MAP
                ELSE IF PROCESS-ADD-CUSTOMER
                    PERFORM 2000-PROCESS-ADD-CUSTOMER
                ELSE IF PROCESS-CHANGE-CUSTOMER
                    PERFORM 3000-PROCESS-CHANGE-CUSTOMER
                ELSE IF PROCESS-DELETE-CUSTOMER
                    PERFORM 4000-PROCESS-DELETE-CUSTOMER
            WHEN OTHER——————————————————————————Other key
                IF PROCESS-KEY-MAP
                    MOVE LOW-VALUE TO MNTMAP10
                    MOVE -1 TO CUSTNO1L
                    MOVE 'That key is unassigned.' TO MSG10
                    SET SEND-DATAONLY-ALARM TO TRUE
                    PERFORM 1500-SEND-KEY-MAP
                ELSE
                    MOVE LOW-VALUE TO MNTMAP20
                    MOVE -1 TO CUSTNO2L
                    MOVE 'That key is unassigned.' TO MSG20
                    SET SEND-DATAONLY-ALARM TO TRUE
                    PERFORM 1400-SEND-CUSTOMER-MAP
        END-EVALUATE.
        EXEC CICS
            RETURN TRANSID('MNT1')
                   COMMAREA(COMMUNICATION-AREA)
        END-EXEC.
```

Figure 5-12   Effective coding for the top module of a CICS program

Edit modules

When you edit the data that's received from a map, you usually want to identify the fields that are invalid when you send the map back to the terminal. You also want to display a message on the screen for at least one of the fields that's invalid. This makes it easier for the user to find and correct the errors.

Figure 5-13 gives a recommended structure for coding an edit module. Here, the fields are tested for validity in reverse order of how they appear on the screen so the error message will be for the first invalid field and the cursor will be positioned at the start of that field. For each field that's invalid, the attribute byte is changed to highlight the field (in this case, reverse display is used); minus one is moved to the length of the field to position the cursor at the start of the field; and a message is moved to the message area.

Coding structure

```
Set default attributes for fields to be edited.
IF error-condition for field-1
    MOVE attribute-character TO attribute-field for field-1
    MOVE -1                  TO length-field for field-1
    MOVE error-message       TO error-message-field
    MOVE 'N' to VALID-DATA-SWITCH.
IF error-condition for field-2
    MOVE attribute-character TO attribute-field for field-2
    MOVE -1                  TO length-field for field-2
    MOVE error-message       TO error-message-field
    MOVE 'N' to VALID-DATA-SWITCH.
IF error-condition for field-3
    .
    .
```

Coding example

```
2200-EDIT-CUSTOMER-DATA.
*
    MOVE ATTR-NO-HIGHLIGHT TO ZIPCODEH
                             STATEH
                             CITYH
                             ADDRH
                             FNAMEH
                             LNAMEH.
    IF      ZIPCODEI = SPACE
        OR ZIPCODEL = ZERO
        MOVE ATTR-REVERSE TO ZIPCODEH
        MOVE -1 TO ZIPCODEL
        MOVE 'You must enter a zip code.' TO MSG20
        MOVE 'N' TO VALID-DATA-SWITCH.
    IF      STATEI = SPACE
        OR STATEL = ZERO
        MOVE ATTR-REVERSE TO STATEH
        MOVE -1 TO STATEL
        MOVE 'You must enter a state.' TO MSG20
        MOVE 'N' TO VALID-DATA-SWITCH.
    IF      CITYI = SPACE
        OR CITYL = ZERO
        .
        .
```

Notes

- The fields should be tested in the reverse order of how they appear on the screen. That way, the error message that's displayed will be for the first invalid field on the screen and the cursor will be located at the start of that field.

- In the coding example, reverse display is used for each of the invalid fields.

- An edit module like the one in the coding example would probably call subprograms to edit the state and zip code fields. Those calls are omitted to simplify this example.

Figure 5-13   An effective coding structure for an edit module

Unrecoverable CICS errors

Most COBOL shops have standards for handling unrecoverable CICS errors. Often, these standards include starting a separate program for handling the errors. This error-handling program usually displays an error message on the user's terminal, writes detailed error information to an error log, reverses any changes that were made to recoverable files, produces a storage dump, and abends the program.

Figure 5-14 presents coding that can be used for starting an error-handling program when an unrecoverable error is detected. The first surprise is that you use a GO TO statement to branch to the module that invokes the error-handling program and terminates the interactive program. That's the most practical way to do this. To try to do this in a strictly structured way (no GOTOs) just isn't worth the effort since the program isn't going to reach its normal conclusion anyway.

The second surprise is that the terminate module isn't shown on the structure chart for the program. That too is practical for two reasons. First, if you did add this module to the structure chart, it would have to be called by every module that includes a CICS command, which would clutter the chart unnecessarily. Second, this module doesn't actually represent a function that needs to be done by the program. It is only used when an unrecoverable error occurs, which you hope never happens.

If you want to see how the terminate module can be used in an interactive program, please refer to model program 4. There you can see that each module that uses a CICS command to perform a disk operation branches to the terminate module when an unrecoverable error is detected. These are modules 1300, 2300, 3100, 3200, and 4100 in figure 5-10.

A COPY member for error parameters

```
01   ERROR-PARAMETERS.
*
     05   ERR-RESP          PIC S9(8)      COMP.
     05   ERR-RESP2         PIC S9(8)      COMP.
     05   ERR-TRNID         PIC X(4).
     05   ERR-RSRCE         PIC X(8).
```

Invoking an error handling program named SYSERR

```
          .
          .
          IF RESPONSE-CODE NOT = DFHRESP(NORMAL)
              GO TO 9999-TERMINATE-PROGRAM.
          .
          .
*
 9999-TERMINATE-PROGRAM.
*
     MOVE EIBRESP  TO ERR-RESP.
     MOVE EIBRESP2 TO ERR-RESP2.
     MOVE EIBTRNID TO ERR-TRNID.
     MOVE EIBRSRCE TO ERR-RSRCE.
     EXEC CICS
         XCTL PROGRAM("SYSERR")
              COMMAREA(ERROR-PARAMETERS)
     END-EXEC.
```

Notes

- Most COBOL shops have an error handling program that can be used when an unrecoverable error occurs in a CICS program. The most practical way to get to the module that starts this program is to use a GO TO statement as shown above.

- The module that starts the error handling program (module 9999 above) moves fields from the Execute Interface Block to the error parameters area of Working Storage. Then, a CICS XCTL command is used to start the error handling program and pass the error parameters to the program.

- Because the terminate module isn't actually a function of the program, you don't have to include it in the structure chart. If you did, the module would have to be subordinate to every module that uses a CICS command.

- The IF statement in this example shows how the DFHRESP keyword can be used in a CICS program to detect CICS conditions. This keyword became available with CICS version 1.7. Without it, you have to use the CICS HANDLE CONDITION command to detect conditions.

Figure 5-14   Effective coding for handling unrecoverable CICS errors

HANDLE AID and HANDLE CONDITION commands

The CICS HANDLE AID and HANDLE CONDITION commands have implied GOTOs within their syntax. This means that you can't code a module that includes one of these commands as a single COBOL paragraph. Instead, to retain the principles of structured coding, you have to code these modules as sections as shown in figure 5-15. That in turn means that the entire program should be divided into sections, and each module on the structure chart should be coded as a section.

Although you can do an excellent job of developing CICS programs that way, it's usually better to avoid the use of the HANDLE AID and HANDLE CONDITION commands. You can do that if you're using CICS release 1.7 or later. Then, to handle the AID keys, you can use the EIBAID field as shown in figure 5-12. To handle the conditions that result after a CICS I/O operation, you can use the DFHRESP keyword in an IF statement. This is illustrated in figure 5-14 and also by the code for modules 2300, 3100, 3200, and 4100 in model program 4. Since these alternatives eliminate the need for sections and GO TO statements, this is the preferred method for structured coding.

Another reason for avoiding the use of the HANDLE AID command is that it forces you to issue a RECEIVE MAP command just to detect the use of an attention key. In many cases, though, you don't need the data received from the map to process the attention key. Then, issuing a RECEIVE MAP command wastes processing time. If, for example, the user presses the PF3 key to end the program, it can be handled by the top module as shown in figure 5-12 without receiving the map.

The last reason for not using the HANDLE AID command is that it drives the event-driven logic of your program deeper into the program's structure. Instead of detecting the use of the PF3 key in the top module, for example, a module in one of the lower levels has to detect it. But that usually means that more switches or flags have to be used, which complicates the coding of the program and makes it more difficult to read. This is perhaps the most compelling reason for avoiding the use of he HANDLE AID command.

If you do have to use HANDLE AID or HANDLE CONDITION, though, figure 5-15 shows a coding structure that makes the use of these commands manageable. Note that each section has only one entry and one exit when coded this way so you still adhere to the principles of structured programming. For consistency, the other modules of the program should also be coded as sections, and those modules shouldn't contain any paragraph names. That way, all of the PERFORM statements in the program refer to section names, and none refer to paragraph names.

Coding structure

```
xxxx-module-name SECTION.
*
     HANDLE AID or HANDLE CONDITION command.
     CICS command that requires the HANDLE command.
     GO TO xxxx-EXIT.
*
xxxx-routine-1.
*
     COBOL statements for key-or-condition-1.
     GO TO xxxx-EXIT.
*
xxxx-routine-2.
*
     .
     .
*
xxxx-EXIT.
*
     EXIT.
```

Coding example that uses the **HANDLE AID** command

```
2100-RECEIVE-CUSTOMER-MAP SECTION.
*
     EXEC CICS
         HANDLE AID CLEAR(2100-CLEAR-KEY)
                    ANYKEY(2100-ANYKEY)
     END-EXEC.
     EXEC CICS
         RECEIVE MAP("MNTMAP2")
                 MAPSET("MNTSET1")
                 INTO(MNTMAP2I)
     END-EXEC.
     GO TO 2100-EXIT.
*
2100-CLEAR-KEY.
*
     MOVE "Y" TO CANCEL-ENTRY-SWITCH.
     GO TO 2100-EXIT.
*
2100-ANYKEY.
*
     MOVE "N" TO VALID-DATA-SWITCH.
     MOVE "INVALID KEY PRESSED" TO MSG20.
     MOVE -1 TO NAMEL.
*
2100-EXIT.
*
     EXIT.
```

Notes

- If you're using CICS release 1.7 or later, you can avoid the use of the HANDLE AID and HANDLE CONDITION commands by using the EIBAID field for handling AID keys and by using the DFHRESP keyword for handling error conditions.

- If you do use the HANDLE AID or HANDLE CONDITION command, the module that contains it should be coded as a section as shown above. Then, it makes sense to code all of the modules of the program as sections.

Figure 5-15   An effective coding structure for the HANDLE AID or HANDLE CONDITION command

Perspective

This chapter shows how the principles of structured design and structured coding can be applied to interactive programs. Because these programs tend to be longer and more complicated than batch programs, structured methods are especially valuable when applied to interactive programs. Similarly, since CICS increases the design and coding complexity of an interactive program, structured methods are even more valuable for CICS programs.

Summary

- An event/response chart summarizes the *events* that a terminal user can initiate from each of the *contexts* of an interactive session. The *response* is the processing that the program does for each event. This type of chart can help you plan the design and coding of a program.

- When you design an interactive program, the primary module in the second level of the chart should call modules that represent the major contexts of the program or the major responses to the events of the program. In addition, the module names should reflect the event-driven nature of the program.

- Most interactive programs for mid-range systems or PC networks display or accept an entire *screen* of data with a single COBOL statement. In these programs, it makes sense to isolate the ACCEPT statements in their own modules.

- In contrast to the *conversational processing* of other types of interactive programs, CICS programs use *pseudo-conversational processing*. This means the CICS program ends each time that a *map* is sent to a user's terminal. This type of processing improves the overall efficiency of a CICS system.

- When you use pseudo-conversational processing, there's one less level in the design of the program because the top module represents the processing for the data that's received from just one map.

- Because CICS complicates the coding of an interactive program, it's even more important to use structured coding in the Data Division, in the top module of the Procedure Division, and in the edit modules. In addition, you need a consistent way to handle unrecoverable errors.

- If you have to use the HANDLE AID or HANDLE CONDITION command in a CICS program, you are forced to use sections and GO TO statements. Then, each module of the structure chart should be coded as a section.

Chapter 6

The 10 most-frequently asked questions

1. *What difference does it make if the modules in a chart represent functions as long as the modules can be coded without GOTOs?*

2. *Speaking as a manager, how much will my programmers improve if they use your methods?*

3. *What difference does it make if each module is functionally subordinate to the module that calls it as long as the code doesn't use GOTOs?*

4. *What do you do if your boss doesn't use the methods of this book?*

5. *How can I make use of your methods when I have to maintain old programs that weren't written that way?*

6. *What's wrong with an occasional GO TO statement?*

7. *What's wrong with using other types of diagrams or charts when you design a program?*

8. *As a manager, how can I get my programmers to use your methods for developing COBOL programs?*

9. *How much will I improve if I use your methods?*

10. *What do you call your methods?*

During the last 20 years, Paul Noll has given his seminars to hundreds of programmers and we've received hundreds of letters from people who've read the first editions of this book. What follows are 10 of the questions that are asked the most along with Paul's answers.

1. What difference does it make if the modules in a chart represent functions as long as the modules can be coded without GOTOs?

Figure 6-1 presents a structure chart for a program that prepares a simple report with summarized totals for salesreps (the first control break) and branches (the second control break). Some of the modules in this chart clearly don't represent functions (like 500-BRANCH-BREAK and 600-SALESREP-BREAK), and you can't tell whether some of the other modules are functional because none of the module names describe functions. Now, what's wrong with that?

The problem is that there's no logical way of creating a structure chart like this one without having a pretty good idea of how you're going to code the program first. And that defeats the purpose of using the structure chart as a design tool. In contrast, focusing on the program functions gives you a logical way of dividing a large programming problem into manageable modules, which makes coding the program significantly easier. And that's what's needed in the real world of production programming.

Incidentally, we didn't just make up the structure chart in this figure. It is adapted from a chart in a COBOL textbook that's used in dozens of college and community college courses. When we analyzed this chart, we had a hard time figuring out the logic behind it. Branch-break and salesrep-break modules subordinate to a calc-routine module? That doesn't make sense. Branch-break and salesrep-break modules treated as common modules that appear in two or three places in the same program. Wow!

In fact, you can only understand a program with a chart like this after you look at its code. That's why we've included some of the code in figure 6-2. Once you understand the code, the chart starts to make sense. Obviously, though, this should work the other way around. The chart should be the index to the code.

2. Speaking as a manager, how much will my programmers improve if they use your methods?

Paul usually answers a question like this with a question: "How do you measure how your programmers are doing now?" In most cases, the manager appears startled, then stammers out an answer that shows that his company doesn't measure programmer productivity, program reliability, or program maintainability. In that case, Paul says, "It's not going to matter how much they're going to improve because you won't know about it anyway."

If you do measure the work of your programmers, though, the answer to this question depends on the methods you're using now. If your programmers develop charts like the one in figure 6-1, the improvements should be substantial. And if your programmers "compose" at the terminal without ever designing, the improvements should be dramatic.

A structure chart for a program that prepares a summary report by salesrep within branch

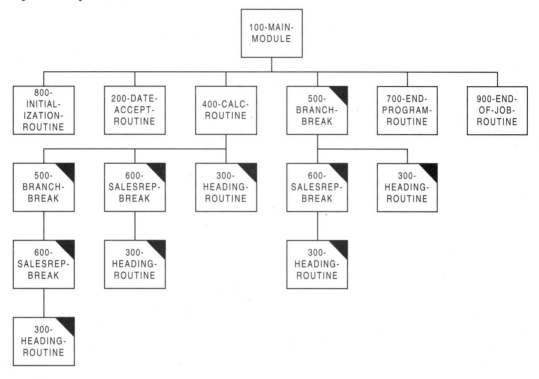

Problems

- How do you design a chart like this from the top down? What's the logic behind the design process?

- On what basis or using what logic does it make sense for the branch-break and salesrep-break modules to be subordinate to the calc-routine module? Or for the branch-break module to also be subordinate to the main-module module?

- How can you tell what code each module includes? For instance, what module do you think contains the primary control code for the program? What module do you think contains the READ statement for the input file? What module do you think contains the CLOSE statement for the files?

Figure 6-1   A structure chart with modules that aren't independent functions

3. What difference does it make if each module is functionally subordinate to the module that calls it as long as the code doesn't use GOTOs?

In the chart in figure 6-1 and the code in figure 6-2, several of the modules aren't functionally subordinate to the modules that call them. For instance, the salesrep-break and branch-break modules aren't functionally subordinate to the calc-routine module. When that happens, you can't understand the program just by reading it from the top down. Instead, you have to study the code in several modules to see how they're related.

If you read the code for the top module in figure 6-2, for example, it's hard to guess what module 400 does or how it can be driven by the NOT AT END clause in the READ statement. Then, when you read the code for module 400, it's not clear why that module has to perform module 300 when module 300 is also performed by modules 500 and 600 and those modules are called from module 000. It's only after you see how all the modules are related that you can understand the code.

When you code this way, the coding takes longer, there's more chance for bugs, and you can't get the benefits that top-down testing offers. And after the program goes into production, maintenance becomes far more difficult than it ought to be. If that isn't obvious in this simple example, try it with a 10,000 line interactive program.

4. What do you do if your boss doesn't use the methods of this book?

That depends on whether she cares how you design and code *your* programs. If she doesn't, just use the methods in this book until someone questions them. In time, you may be able to show that you get more done in less time with programs that have fewer bugs. That may get her interested in your methods.

If your boss actually prohibits the use of the methods in this book, that's a serious problem and one that we've been asked about many times during the last 20 years. Then, you've got several alternatives, and none are that good. You can do the work your boss's way while knowing you can do better (not an easy thing to do and one that will make you crazy if it goes on too long). You can ask your boss for a pilot project that will give you a chance to demonstrate the effectiveness of your methods. You can give your boss a copy of this book to help convince her that the entire shop ought to change its methods. And when all else fails, you can look for another job, but this time make sure that methods are discussed during the employment interviews. This is truly a nasty problem, though, and we by no means make light of it.

The code for the opening modules of the program that's charted in figure 6-1

```
****************************************************************
 PROCEDURE DIVISION.
 100-MAIN-MODULE.
     PERFORM 800-INITIALIZATION-ROUTINE
     PERFORM 200-DATE-ACCEPT-ROUTINE
     PERFORM UNTIL NO-MORE-RECORDS
         READ CUSTMAST
             AT END
                 MOVE "NO" TO ARE-THERE-MORE-RECORDS
             NOT AT END
                 PERFORM 400-CALC-ROUTINE
         END-READ
     END-PERFORM
     PERFORM 500-BRANCH-BREAK
     PERFORM 700-END-PROGRAM-ROUTINE
     PERFORM 900-END-OF-JOB-ROUTINE
     STOP RUN.
****************************************************************
        .
        .
        .
****************************************************************
 400-CALC-ROUTINE.
     EVALUATE TRUE
         WHEN FIRST-RECORD = "YES"
             MOVE CM-BRANCH-NUMBER TO OLD-BRANCH-NUMBER
             MOVE CM-SALESREP-NUMBER TO OLD-SALESREP-NUMBER
             PERFORM 300-HEADING-ROUTINE
             MOVE "NO" TO FIRST-RECORD
         WHEN CM-BRANCH-NUMBER NOT = OLD-BRANCH-NUMBER
             PERFORM 500-BRANCH-BREAK
         WHEN CM-SALESREP-NUMBER NOT = OLD-SALESREP-NUMBER
             PERFORM 600-SALESREP-BREAK
     END-EVALUATE
     IF WS-LINE-CTR IS GREATER THAN 55
         PERFORM 300-HEADING-ROUTINE
     END-IF
        .
        .
****************************************************************
 500-BRANCH-BREAK.
     PERFORM 600-SALESREP-BREAK
        .
        .
****************************************************************
 600-SALESREP-BREAK.
        .
        .
```

Problems

- You can't understand one module of the program at a time by reading the code from the top down. Instead, you have to read the code in several modules before you understand how the interrelationships work.

- Although the dependent relationships between modules are tolerable in a simple report preparation program like this one, they become overwhelming in a large program.

Figure 6-2   Code for a program with modules that aren't independent functions

5. How can I make use of your methods when I have to maintain old programs that weren't written that way?

The programs in the real world are often far worse than the one in figures 6-1 and 6-2. For rookies, the code in figure 6-3 gives you some idea of what you might run into. These are actual examples taken from production programs in the 1980s, and any programmer who has done maintenance work can probably tell you about programs that are just as bad or worse.

Figure 6-3 gives you some ideas of how you can use our methods when you maintain unstructured or poorly structured programs. In all cases, the key ingredient is common sense. Since your goal is usually to debug or maintain the program in the quickest way possible, you can't afford to restructure the entire program or rewrite large portions of code. Instead, you have to focus on just those portions of the program that you have to change. Then, you can apply our methods to those portions of code as you make the changes.

That's not much of an answer, I know. What's worse, the answer will be just as bad 10 years from now unless your COBOL shop adopts standards now that will make the programs easier to maintain then.

6. What's wrong with an occasional GO TO statement?

The short answer is that there's not much wrong with it. If you look at figure 5-14, for example, you can see that we recommend the use of GO TO statements in the case of unrecoverable errors in CICS programs. Although you can write these programs so they don't contain any GOTOs, that would be more trouble than it's worth. In this case, practicality is more sensible than structured programming purism.

You can make similar cases for other uses of GO TO statements. The trouble is that one programmer says "I like to use a GO TO statement in the primary module in the second level to branch to the end of the module on an end-of-file condition." Okay. Then, another programmer wants to use GOTOs for another purpose, a third for a third purpose, and so on. If you allow all these uses, the coding consistency from one program to another breaks down, and you start to lose the benefits that the consistent use of structured programming standards promises.

A coding sample from an actual production program

```
AA43.   PERFORM KK.
        IF ITMSTS20 = " " GO TO AAA43.
        IF ITMSTS20 = "N" AND ITMSTS0 (A, SS) = "N".
        PERFORM A54G THRU X546 GO TO B43.
        IF ITMSTS20 = "N" PERFORM CC43 PERFORM A54J.
        MOVE "25" TO ACT40 MOVE ITMSTS20 TO ITMSTS40 GO TO B43.
        IF ITMSTS70 (A, SS) = "N" GO TO CC43.
AAA43.  PERFORM EQCHEC.
        IF EQWORK1 = EQWORK2 GO TO QQ43.
        IF EQWORK2 = SPACES GO TO QQ43.
        GO TO CC43.
QQ43.   PERFORM EE THRU KK.
B43.    PERFORM A54D THRU X54D GO TO D42.
CC43.   MOVE "40" TO ACT40.
          .
          .
```

A coding sample from one program in an expensive software package

```
LEVEL-1 SECTION.
MAIN-LOGIC.
    PERFORM OPENING-PROCEDURE.
    IF OPENING-PROCEDURE-SUCCESSFUL
        IF PR-CTL-USE-JOB-NUMBER-FLAG IS = "N"
            PERFORM JOB-NOS-NOT-SELECTED-MESSAGE,
            MOVE UNSUCCESSFUL TO OPENING-PROCEDURE-STATUS,
        ELSE
            PERFORM ENTER-MENU-SELECTION,
            IF NOT END-KEY-PRESSED
                PERFORM JOB-FILE-MAINTENANCE UNTIL
                END-KEY-PRESSED.
    PERFORM CLOSING-PROCEDURE.
MAIN-LOGIC-EXIT.
    PERFORM WAIT-MESSAGE-ROUTINE.
    EXIT PROGRAM.
    STOP RUN.
LEVEL-2 SECTION.
OPENING PROCEDURE.
      .
      .
```

Guidelines for maintaining a "legacy" program

- Get all the documentation you can find. Then, if necessary, try to get more information from anyone else who's worked on the program.

- Print the source file so you know what the latest version of the program is. If necessary, sketch out a structure chart for the program or generate a structure listing from the source code.

- Isolate the portions of the program that need to be changed and use the methods of this book to design, code, and test the changes.

- Do *not* change portions of the program that don't need to be changed just to make the program easier to maintain the next time.

Figure 6-3   How to apply the methods of this book when you maintain old programs

7. What's wrong with using other types of diagrams or charts when you design a program?

Figure 6-4 presents two of the several graphic forms that can be used for the design of a program, and the short answer is that there's not much wrong with using these graphic forms. In particular, a Warnier-Orr diagram has some benefits since it can be drawn quickly by hand. In effect, it's a structure chart drawn sideways without the boxes.

Remember, though, that the graphic methods have little to do with program design. The critical issues are what each module represents, how you design the subordinate levels for each module, how long you continue the division process, whether Read and Write functions are isolated in separate modules, how you name the modules, and so on. These are the issues that determine whether your design methods are going to be effective, and that's what's wrong with the designs in figure 6-4.

From a practical point of view, it also makes sense to spend as little time on graphics as possible since that has nothing to do with the design. As a result, you don't want to make the graphics too fancy or add time-consuming details like what data or switches are passed from one module to another. You just want to show what the modules are and what the relationships between the modules are.

8. As a manager, how can I get my programmers to use your methods for developing COBOL programs?

First, you have to set standards for the design, coding, and testing methods that the programmers in a shop are supposed to use. Then, you have to enforce the use of those standards. Although most COBOL shops set standards in the 80s, not many shops enforced their use, and that's one reason why we have most of the same problems today that we had then.

If you decide now that you would like to change your shop standards to the ones in this book, you can start by buying this book for each staff member and saying that these are now your standards. To help make this work, we've deliberately kept the recommendations in this book to a minimum. That makes these standards easier to teach and enforce.

If you don't think a book is going to convince your staff that it's time to change their design and development methods, another alternative is to hire a consultant (like Paul Noll) to train your staff. Often, an outsider who specializes in a subject can be more convincing than insiders. But whether you use our books or a consultant, don't limit the training to programmers; include the analysts and the managers so they can support the new methods too.

Once your programmers believe in the methods and know what the standards are, you can enforce them in several ways. You can review the design and coding of the programs yourself. You can set up peer reviews. Or you can set up

A Warnier-Orr diagram for model program 1

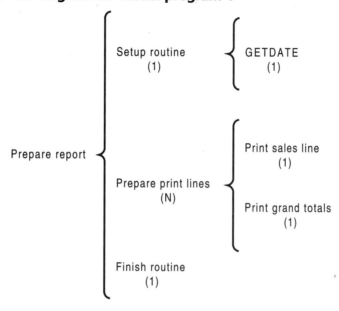

A tree chart for model program 1

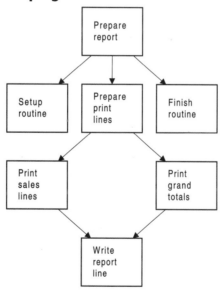

Problems

- Neither one of the designs shown above conforms to the design standards presented in this book. That's the issue that matters.

- The differences in the graphics are trivial. However, a Warnier-Orr diagram becomes difficult to work with after just a few levels to the right. And a tree chart often becomes unwieldy when you draw lines to common modules.

more formal reviews that you attend. This is particularly important in the first few months after you change the standards and during the first few months that a new programmer is on the job.

I know, I know, you don't have the time to review the code and neither do your programmers because you're all on impossible schedules. But someone has to do it if you want programming to improve in your shop. The good news is that reviews are actually a form of training, and the payback potential is enormous.

9. How much will I improve if I use your methods?

If your manager doesn't measure your productivity, you probably don't either. But why not start? If you do, you'll clearly see improvement. How much depends on how bad your methods were before. To double your productivity, though, wouldn't be unusual.

Even if you don't measure the results, you'll "know" that you've improved because you'll feel more in control than ever before. To give you some idea of what you can expect, figure 6-5 presents excerpts from some of the many letters we've received from programmers during the last 20 years. In most cases, these programmers didn't actually measure the changes in their work, but they "knew" that they were doing better work than ever before.

10. What do you call your methods?

Way back in the 1970s, when every structured programming promoter had a special name for his methods (they were all men in those days), a programmer in one of Paul's seminars asked what his methods were called. When Paul said he didn't call them anything, the programmer said "But you have to have a name for your methods or they won't become popular." Then, he thought for a while and said "How about 'Paul Noll's functional decomposition'?"

Today, Paul still doesn't have a special name for his methods. He just uses the generic names: structured design, structured coding, and top-down testing. Since Paul's methods are actually a composite of ideas taken from many sources, those generic names are both appropriate and adequate. What we hope we've done in this book is to give you specific meanings and useful methods for each of those generic names.

How our methods have worked for other people

"My project manager wanted me to learn structured programming, so I read your book and the first structured program I wrote, albeit simple, ran the first time, like a champ!"

> Systems Engineer
> Philadelphia, PA

"[Using Paul's methods,] a project I just finished specifying a month or two ago is already nearing the unit testing stage; i.e., we are 45 days ahead of schedule!"

> Project Controller
> Cleveland, OH

"Your structured programming concepts made a lot of sense. Almost overnight my coding style has improved."

> Programmer
> West Bend, WI

"I have been using the principles in your books for about six months now with much satisfaction. I'm convinced that no one else has come out with specific and yet practical standards for COBOL programming like your books by Noll have done."

> Programmer/Analyst
> Portland, OR

"Your book has stopped the re-invention of programs and has helped to promote the sharing of code and ideas."

> Projects Manager
> Little Rock, AR

"The first thing I've seen in print that was really useful for the COBOL programmer who wants to write structured code."

> Programmer
> Hartford, CT

"Great book! My co-workers won't let me have it back."

> Programmer
> Eugene, OR

"An excellent book! I have read other books on structured programming but none of them carried the structured theme through the design and test stage. Your book was very easy to follow and understand. The numerous examples were very helpful."

> Programmer/Analyst
> Bismarck, ND

"We found this book extremely useful and are adopting it as a programming standard in our shop."

> Director of Program Development
> Providence, RI

"Prior to receiving this book, I had spent considerable time reading and researching structured programming, but I had found trying to implement any form of standards (in our 95% COBOL shop) a fruitless adventure. In the last three months with the aid of this book, we have installed our version of structured COBOL programming and we are thoroughly convinced the benefits we receive are immeasurable."

> Programmer/Analyst
> Omaha, NE

"Your structured programming books are very helpful, even though I've had to modify some of the concepts in order to conform to installation standards. Until I read your book, I had always regarded structured programming as something that was nice in theory, but impractical to implement."

> Programmer
> Foxboro, MA

"After reading your books for two hours, I was convinced that I never knew how to write a good COBOL program, and I promptly became a convert."

> Professor
> Pittsfield, MA

Figure 6-5   What programmers have said during the last 20 years

```
  PROCEDURE DIVISION.
*
  000-PREPARE-SALES-REPORT.
*
      OPEN INPUT  CUSTMAST
                  BRCHMAST
                  SALESRPT
      PERFORM  0-FORMAT-REPORT
      PERFORM  0-LOAD-BRANCH-T
      PERFORM 300-PREPARE-SALES
          UNTIL
      PERFORM
      CLOSE CUSTMAST
            BRCHMAST


      STOP RUN
*
```

Section 2

Model programs

This section presents five model programs. They are in sequence (1) a report preparation program, (2) a random update program, (3) an interactive file maintenance program in Micro Focus COBOL, (4) an interactive file maintenance program that uses CICS on a mainframe, and (5) a report preparation program that uses DB2 and embedded SQL on a mainframe.

Each of the programs has been simplified, of course, so the essential structure and coding of the program is easier to read and understand. The documentation for each program includes the program specifications, COPY members, subprogram descriptions, report and screen layouts when necessary, structure chart, and COBOL source listing.

The intent of these programs is to serve as models for the development of new programs. If, for example, you're about to write a report preparation program, you can start by reviewing the structure chart and code for the model report preparation program. Then, you can copy the code that you want to reuse from the model program to the new program.

Often, you may want to copy code from more than one model program as you create a new program. If, for example, you're developing an interactive update program that requires the use of a table, you can copy the bulk of the code from one of the interactive model programs and the table handling code from the report preparation program.

After you work this way for a while, you'll build your own library of model programs. These models will be more realistic because they will be actual production programs. They will also reflect your own coding practices so you'll enjoy using them more than our models.

Program 1

This model program prepares a simple sales report with intermediate totals for each branch and grand totals at the end of the report. As simple as it is, though, this type of program frequently gave unstructured programmers fits. That was particularly true when the program printed intermediate totals at two or more levels (like salesrep and branch totals).

In contrast to unstructured programs, all of the critical logic of this model program is concentrated in just two of the paragraphs in the Procedure Division. In paragraph 300, nested IFs are used to determine when each type of line should be written. This paragraph uses a control field to determine when the branch number changes and branch totals should be printed. Then, module 320 uses nested IFs and the same control field to determine when to get the branch name for the next branch and when to suppress the printing of the branch number and name.

When you concentrate the logic like that, it's easy to modify a program. If, for example, you want to add intermediate totals by salesrep to the report, you can just expand the nested IFs in paragraphs 300 and 320 and add another paragraph to the program for printing the salesrep lines.

Program specifications

Program name	MKTG1200	Page	1
Program description	Prepare Sales Report	Date	11/20/96

Input/output specifications

File name	Description	Format	Use
CUSTMAST	Customer master file	Sequential	Input
BRCHMAST	Branch master file	Sequential	Input
SALESRPT	Sales report	Print file	Output

Processing specifications

- The customer master file is in sequence by customer number within salesrep number within branch number. As the file is read, one line should be printed for each record in the file.

- The branch master file contains 100 or fewer records that are in sequence by branch number. These records should be loaded into a table at the start of the program. This table should then be used to get the branch name for each group of customer records.

- Sales totals should be kept for each branch, and a total line should be printed for each branch when the group of customer records for one branch ends and the group for the next branch begins.

- At the end of the report, a grand total for each sales column should be printed.

Note

- The specifications say that the branch table should be loaded at the start of the program and searched whenever the program needs to get the next branch name. Although you probably wouldn't do it that way in a production program, we wrote the program specifications like that so one of the model programs would include table-handling modules.

COPY members

CUSTMAST

```
01   CUSTOMER-MASTER-RECORD.
*
     05   CM-BRANCH-NUMBER        PIC XX.
     05   CM-SALESREP-NUMBER      PIC XX.
     05   CM-CUSTOMER-NUMBER      PIC X(5).
     05   CM-CUSTOMER-NAME        PIC X(20).
     05   CM-SALES-THIS-YTD       PIC S9(5)V99.
     05   CM-SALES-LAST-YTD       PIC S9(5)V99.
     05   FILLER                  PIC X(5).
```

BRCHMAST

```
01   BRANCH-MASTER-RECORD.
*
     05   BM-BRANCH-NUMBER        PIC XX.
     05   BM-BRANCH-NAME          PIC X(18).
```

Notes

- The record layouts are intentionally simplified so the emphasis is on the structure and logic of the program, not on data manipulation.

- In actual practice, the definitions for the numeric fields in the disk records would probably include COMP-3 or PACKED-DECIMAL usage.

Subprogram

GETDATE

This subprogram gets the current date and time. To use it, you must pass a 10-character date and a 8-character time field to it. The date and time are returned in a format that's ready for use in the heading of a report.

Sample report

```
DATE:   01/24/1997              MIKE MURACH & ASSOCIATES, INC.                    PAGE:     1
TIME:   10:23 AM                                                                 MKTG1200
                                  YEAR-TO-DATE SALES REPORT

BRCH                    CUST                        SALES          SALES       CHANGE      CHANGE
NO    BRANCH NAME       NO     CUSTOMER NAME       THIS YTD       LAST YTD     AMOUNT       PCT.

12    FORT WAYNE        11111  INFORMATION BUILDERS  1,234.56      1,111.11      123.45     11.1
                        12345  CAREER TRAINING CTR  12,345.67     22,222.22    9,876.55-   44.4-

                               BRANCH TOTALS:       13,580.23     23,333.33    9,753.10-   41.8-

22    MILWAUKEE CENTRAL 22222  HOMELITE TEXTRON CO  34,545.00        100.00   34,445.00   OVRFLW
                        34567  NEAS MEMBER BENEFITS     111.11         0.00      111.11     N/A
                        55555  PILOT LIFE INS. CO.   1,000.00        100.00      900.00    900.0

                               BRANCH TOTALS:       35,656.11        200.00   35,456.11   OVRFLW

34    ST. PAUL          00111  DAUPHIN DEPOSIT BANK 14,099.00     19,930.00    5,831.00-   29.3-
                        12345  AIRCRAFT OWNERS ASSC  5,426.12     40,420.00   34,993.88-   86.6-
                        33333  NORFOLK CORP          6,396.35      4,462.88    1,933.47    43.3

                               BRANCH TOTALS:       25,921.47     64,812.88   38,891.41-   60.0-

47    KANSAS CITY NW    12121  GENERAL SERVICES CO. 11,444.00     11,059.56      384.44     3.5
                        22222  INFO MANAGEMENT CO.  17,481.45     11,892.47    5,588.98    47.0
                        33333  DOLLAR SAVINGS BANK   5,059.00      4,621.95      437.05     9.5
                        34567  NATL MUSIC CORP.      2,383.46      4,435.26    2,051.80-   46.3-

                               BRANCH TOTALS:       36,367.91     32,009.24    4,358.67    13.6

                               GRAND TOTALS:       111,525.72    120,355.45    8,829.73-    7.3-
```

Notes

- A sample report is given instead of a report layout so you can see what the printed output is supposed to look like.
- The length of each print line in this report is only 100 characters, instead of the normal 132, so the report can fit vertically on the page in this book.

Structure chart

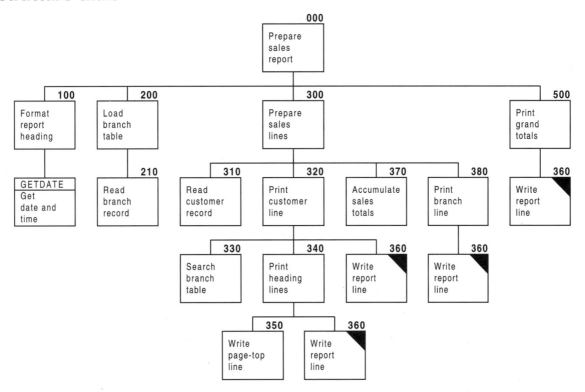

Notes

- Module 320 calls module 340 whenever the line number of the last line printed has reached the maximum number of lines to be printed on a page. Then, module 340 prints the heading lines. To make this work for the first page of the report, appropriate values have to be given to the line-count and lines-on-page fields in working storage. Note that module 340 isn't called by modules 380 or 500 so the report won't be skipped to the next page before branch or grand totals are printed.

- Module 370 accumulates both the branch totals and the grand totals. Another alternative, though, is to accumulate these totals in other modules of the program. In that case, module 370 could be deleted from the structure chart.

Source listing notes

Compiler used

- This program was compiled and tested using the Micro Focus Workbench with the VS COBOL II Version 4.0 compiler options. This compiler supports the 1985 standards.

Working-Storage Section

- The LINE-COUNT and LINES-ON-PAGE fields are used by module 320 to determine whether or not the page is full and heading lines need to be printed on the next page. These fields are initialized with values that cause the headings to be printed on the first page of the report.

200-LOAD-BRANCH-TABLE

- This paragraph uses an in-line PERFORM WITH TEST AFTER and the structured delimiters END-IF and END-PERFORM. If your compiler doesn't support these language elements, you have to use a PERFORM UNTIL in paragraph 000 as shown in figure 2-12.

300-PREPARE-SALES-LINES

- This paragraph uses a FIRST-RECORD-SWITCH so the first record in the file can be processed differently from subsequent records. This paragraph also uses a control field named OLD-BRANCH-NUMBER to determine when the branch number changes.

- This paragraph illustrates the principle of moving the control code up in the structure of the program. Although that may make the coding in this module more complicated, it concentrates the program logic so the program is easier to debug.

320-PRINT-CUSTOMER-LINE

- This paragraph illustrates an extended meaning for the *print* verb. Besides preparing the customer line for printing, this paragraph (1) performs 330-search-branch-table to search for the branch name and (2) computes two of the fields that must be printed. When the customer line is ready for printing, this module checks to see whether the printing has reached the bottom of the current page and calls 340-print-heading-lines if it has. Then, this module calls 360-write-report-line to actually print the customer line on the page.

370-ACCUMULATE-SALES-TOTALS

- This paragraph accumulates the branch totals and the grand totals. This is a simple and direct way to accumulate these totals. A more traditional way to do this is to delete this paragraph, to accumulate the branch totals in paragraph 320, and to accumulate the grand totals in paragraph 380 by summing the branch totals.

380-PRINT-BRANCH-LINE.

- This paragraph, like paragraph 500, illustrates an extended meaning for the verb *print*. Here the module computes two of the fields that must be printed and resets the branch totals to zero.

Source listing

```
        IDENTIFICATION DIVISION.
*
        PROGRAM-ID. MKTG1200.
*
        ENVIRONMENT DIVISION.
*
        INPUT-OUTPUT SECTION.
*
        FILE-CONTROL.
*
            SELECT CUSTMAST ASSIGN TO CUSTMAST.
            SELECT BRCHMAST ASSIGN TO BRCHMAST.
            SELECT SALESRPT ASSIGN TO SALESRPT.
*
        DATA DIVISION.
*
        FILE SECTION.
*
        FD  CUSTMAST
            LABEL RECORDS ARE STANDARD
            RECORD CONTAINS 48 CHARACTERS.
*
            COPY CUSTMAST.
*
        FD  BRCHMAST
            LABEL RECORDS ARE STANDARD
            RECORD CONTAINS 20 CHARACTERS.
*
            COPY BRCHMAST.
*
        FD  SALESRPT
            LABEL RECORDS ARE STANDARD
            RECORD CONTAINS 132 CHARACTERS.
*
        01  PRINT-AREA        PIC X(132).
*
        WORKING-STORAGE SECTION.
*
        01  SWITCHES.
*
            05  FIRST-RECORD-SWITCH       PIC X     VALUE "Y".
                88  FIRST-RECORD                    VALUE "Y".
            05  CUSTMAST-EOF-SWITCH       PIC X     VALUE "N".
                88  CUSTMAST-EOF                    VALUE "Y".
            05  BRCHMAST-EOF-SWITCH       PIC X     VALUE "N".
                88  BRCHMAST-EOF                    VALUE "Y".
*
        01  PRINT-FIELDS          PACKED-DECIMAL.
*
            05  SPACE-CONTROL    PIC S9.
            05  PAGE-COUNT       PIC S9(3)     VALUE ZERO.
            05  LINES-ON-PAGE    PIC S9(3)     VALUE +53.
            05  LINE-COUNT       PIC S9(3)     VALUE +99.
*
        01  DATE-AND-TIME-FIELDS.
*
            05  TODAYS-DATE      PIC X(10).
            05  TODAYS-TIME      PIC X(8).
```

131

```
*
 01   TOTAL-FIELDS                         PACKED-DECIMAL.
*
      05   BRANCH-TOTAL-THIS-YTD     PIC S9(7)V99     VALUE ZERO.
      05   BRANCH-TOTAL-LAST-YTD     PIC S9(7)V99     VALUE ZERO.
      05   GRAND-TOTAL-THIS-YTD      PIC S9(9)V99     VALUE ZERO.
      05   GRAND-TOTAL-LAST-YTD      PIC S9(9)V99     VALUE ZERO.
*
 01   WORK-FIELDS.
*
      05   OLD-BRANCH-NUMBER         PIC XX.
      05   BRANCH-NAME               PIC X(18).
      05   CHANGE-AMOUNT PIC S9(7)V99     VALUE ZERO   PACKED-DECIMAL.
*
 01   BRANCH-TABLE.
*
      05   BT-ENTRIES                OCCURS 100 TIMES
                                     INDEXED BY BT-INDEX.
           10   BT-BRANCH-NUMBER     PIC XX.
           10   BT-BRANCH-NAME       PIC X(18).
      05   BT-ENTRY-COUNT            INDEX.
*
 01   REPORT-TITLE.
*
      05   FILLER       PIC X(17)    VALUE SPACE.
      05   FILLER       PIC X(20)    VALUE "YEAR-TO-DATE SALES R".
      05   FILLER       PIC X(23)    VALUE "EPORT                   ".
*
 01   HEADING-LINE-1.
*
      05   FILLER               PIC X(7)    VALUE "DATE:".
      05   HDG1-DATE            PIC X(10).
      05   FILLER               PIC X(18)   VALUE SPACE.
      05   FILLER               PIC X(15)   VALUE "MIKE MURACH & A".
      05   FILLER               PIC X(15)   VALUE "SSOCIATES, INC.".
      05   FILLER               PIC X(25)   VALUE SPACE.
      05   FILLER               PIC X(6)    VALUE "PAGE:".
      05   HDG1-PAGE-NUMBER     PIC ZZZ9.
      05   FILLER               PIC X(32)   VALUE SPACE.
*
 01   HEADING-LINE-2.
*
      05   FILLER               PIC X(7)    VALUE "TIME:".
      05   HDG2-TIME            PIC X(8).
      05   FILLER               PIC X(75)   VALUE SPACE.
      05   HDG2-REPORT-NUMBER   PIC X(10).
      05   FILLER               PIC X(32)   VALUE SPACE.
*
 01   HEADING-LINE-3.
*
      05   FILLER               PIC X(20)   VALUE SPACE.
      05   HDG3-REPORT-TITLE    PIC X(60).
      05   FILLER               PIC X(52)   VALUE SPACE.
```

```
*
 01    HEADING-LINE-4.
*
       05    FILLER         PIC X(20)     VALUE "BRCH              ".
       05    FILLER         PIC X(20)     VALUE "      CUST         ".
       05    FILLER         PIC X(20)     VALUE "               SAL".
       05    FILLER         PIC X(20)     VALUE "ES      SALES     ".
       05    FILLER         PIC X(20)     VALUE "   CHANGE   CHANGE".
       05    FILLER         PIC X(32)     VALUE SPACE.
*
 01    HEADING-LINE-5.
*
       05    FILLER         PIC X(20)     VALUE " NO   BRANCH NAME    ".
       05    FILLER         PIC X(20)     VALUE "          NO   CUSTOMER".
       05    FILLER         PIC X(20)     VALUE " NAME          THIS".
       05    FILLER         PIC X(20)     VALUE " YTD      LAST YTD ".
       05    FILLER         PIC X(20)     VALUE "    AMOUNT      PCT.".
       05    FILLER         PIC X(32)     VALUE SPACE.
*
 01    CUSTOMER-LINE.
*
       05    FILLER                PIC X         VALUE SPACE.
       05    CL-BRANCH-NUMBER      PIC XX.
       05    FILLER                PIC XX        VALUE SPACE.
       05    CL-BRANCH-NAME        PIC X(18).
       05    FILLER                PIC XX        VALUE SPACE.
       05    CL-CUSTOMER-NUMBER    PIC X(5).
       05    FILLER                PIC XX        VALUE SPACE.
       05    CL-CUSTOMER-NAME      PIC X(20).
       05    FILLER                PIC X(3)      VALUE SPACE.
       05    CL-SALES-THIS-YTD     PIC ZZ,ZZ9.99-.
       05    FILLER                PIC X(4)      VALUE SPACE.
       05    CL-SALES-LAST-YTD     PIC ZZ,ZZ9.99-.
       05    FILLER                PIC X(4)      VALUE SPACE.
       05    CL-CHANGE-AMOUNT      PIC ZZ,ZZ9.99-.
       05    FILLER                PIC X         VALUE SPACE.
       05    CL-CHANGE-PERCENT     PIC ZZ9.9-.
       05    CL-CHANGE-PERCENT-R   REDEFINES CL-CHANGE-PERCENT
                                   PIC X(6).
       05    FILLER                PIC X(32)     VALUE SPACE.
*
 01    BRANCH-LINE.
*
       05    FILLER                PIC X(32)     VALUE SPACE.
       05    FILLER                PIC X(20)     VALUE "BRANCH TOTALS:".
       05    BL-SALES-THIS-YTD     PIC Z,ZZZ,ZZ9.99-.
       05    FILLER                PIC X         VALUE SPACE.
       05    BL-SALES-LAST-YTD     PIC Z,ZZZ,ZZ9.99-.
       05    FILLER                PIC X         VALUE SPACE.
       05    BL-CHANGE-AMOUNT      PIC Z,ZZZ,ZZ9.99-.
       05    FILLER                PIC X         VALUE SPACE.
       05    BL-CHANGE-PERCENT     PIC ZZ9.9-.
       05    BL-CHANGE-PERCENT-R   REDEFINES BL-CHANGE-PERCENT
                                   PIC X(6).
       05    FILLER                PIC X(32)     VALUE SPACE.
```

```
*
 01   GRAND-TOTAL-LINE.
*
     05   FILLER                    PIC X(32)    VALUE SPACE.
     05   FILLER                    PIC X(20)    VALUE "GRAND TOTALS:".
     05   GTL-SALES-THIS-YTD        PIC Z,ZZZ,ZZ9.99-.
     05   FILLER                    PIC X        VALUE SPACE.
     05   GTL-SALES-LAST-YTD        PIC Z,ZZZ,ZZ9.99-.
     05   FILLER                    PIC X        VALUE SPACE.
     05   GTL-CHANGE-AMOUNT         PIC Z,ZZZ,ZZ9.99-.
     05   FILLER                    PIC X        VALUE SPACE.
     05   GTL-CHANGE-PERCENT        PIC ZZ9.9-.
     05   GTL-CHANGE-PERCENT-R      REDEFINES GTL-CHANGE-PERCENT
                                    PIC X(6).
     05   FILLER                    PIC X(32)    VALUE SPACE.
*
 PROCEDURE DIVISION.
*
 000-PREPARE-SALES-REPORT.
*
     OPEN INPUT   CUSTMAST
                  BRCHMAST
            OUTPUT SALESRPT.
     PERFORM 100-FORMAT-REPORT-HEADING.
     PERFORM 200-LOAD-BRANCH-TABLE.
     PERFORM 300-PREPARE-SALES-LINES
         UNTIL CUSTMAST-EOF.
     PERFORM 500-PRINT-GRAND-TOTALS.
     CLOSE CUSTMAST
           BRCHMAST
           SALESRPT.
     STOP RUN.
*
 100-FORMAT-REPORT-HEADING.
*
     CALL "GETDATE" USING TODAYS-DATE TODAYS-TIME.
     MOVE TODAYS-DATE TO HDG1-DATE.
     MOVE TODAYS-TIME TO HDG2-TIME.
     MOVE "MKTG1200"   TO HDG2-REPORT-NUMBER.
     MOVE REPORT-TITLE TO HDG3-REPORT-TITLE.
*
 200-LOAD-BRANCH-TABLE.
*
     PERFORM
         WITH TEST AFTER
         VARYING BT-INDEX FROM 1 BY 1
         UNTIL BRCHMAST-EOF
            OR BT-INDEX = 100
              PERFORM 210-READ-BRANCH-RECORD
              IF NOT BRCHMAST-EOF
                  MOVE BM-BRANCH-NUMBER
                      TO BT-BRANCH-NUMBER (BT-INDEX)
                  MOVE BM-BRANCH-NAME
                      TO BT-BRANCH-NAME (BT-INDEX)
              ELSE
                  SET BT-ENTRY-COUNT TO BT-INDEX
              END-IF
     END-PERFORM.
```

```
*
 210-READ-BRANCH-RECORD.
*
     READ BRCHMAST RECORD
         AT END
             MOVE "Y" TO BRCHMAST-EOF-SWITCH.
*
 300-PREPARE-SALES-LINES.
*
     PERFORM 310-READ-CUSTOMER-RECORD.
     IF NOT CUSTMAST-EOF
         IF FIRST-RECORD
             MOVE CM-BRANCH-NUMBER TO OLD-BRANCH-NUMBER
             PERFORM 320-PRINT-CUSTOMER-LINE
             PERFORM 370-ACCUMULATE-SALES-TOTALS
             MOVE "N" TO FIRST-RECORD-SWITCH
         ELSE
             IF CM-BRANCH-NUMBER = OLD-BRANCH-NUMBER
                 PERFORM 320-PRINT-CUSTOMER-LINE
                 PERFORM 370-ACCUMULATE-SALES-TOTALS
             ELSE
                 PERFORM 380-PRINT-BRANCH-LINE
                 PERFORM 320-PRINT-CUSTOMER-LINE
                 PERFORM 370-ACCUMULATE-SALES-TOTALS
                 MOVE CM-BRANCH-NUMBER TO OLD-BRANCH-NUMBER
     ELSE
         PERFORM 380-PRINT-BRANCH-LINE.
*
 310-READ-CUSTOMER-RECORD.
*
     READ CUSTMAST
         AT END
             MOVE "Y" TO CUSTMAST-EOF-SWITCH.
*
 320-PRINT-CUSTOMER-LINE.
*
     IF FIRST-RECORD
         MOVE CM-BRANCH-NUMBER TO CL-BRANCH-NUMBER
         PERFORM 330-SEARCH-BRANCH-TABLE
         MOVE BRANCH-NAME TO CL-BRANCH-NAME
     ELSE
         IF CM-BRANCH-NUMBER > OLD-BRANCH-NUMBER
             MOVE CM-BRANCH-NUMBER TO CL-BRANCH-NUMBER
             PERFORM 330-SEARCH-BRANCH-TABLE
             MOVE BRANCH-NAME TO CL-BRANCH-NAME
         ELSE
             MOVE SPACE TO CL-BRANCH-NAME
                           CL-BRANCH-NUMBER.
     MOVE CM-CUSTOMER-NUMBER   TO CL-CUSTOMER-NUMBER.
     MOVE CM-CUSTOMER-NAME     TO CL-CUSTOMER-NAME.
     MOVE CM-SALES-THIS-YTD    TO CL-SALES-THIS-YTD.
     MOVE CM-SALES-LAST-YTD    TO CL-SALES-LAST-YTD.
     COMPUTE CHANGE-AMOUNT =
         CM-SALES-THIS-YTD - CM-SALES-LAST-YTD.
     MOVE CHANGE-AMOUNT        TO CL-CHANGE-AMOUNT.
     IF CM-SALES-LAST-YTD NOT EQUAL ZERO
         COMPUTE CL-CHANGE-PERCENT ROUNDED =
             CHANGE-AMOUNT / CM-SALES-LAST-YTD * 100
             ON SIZE ERROR
                 MOVE "OVRFLW" TO CL-CHANGE-PERCENT-R
         END-COMPUTE
```

```
            ELSE
                MOVE "   N/A"              TO CL-CHANGE-PERCENT-R.
            IF LINE-COUNT GREATER LINES-ON-PAGE
                PERFORM 340-PRINT-HEADING-LINES.
            MOVE CUSTOMER-LINE TO PRINT-AREA.
            PERFORM 360-WRITE-REPORT-LINE.
            MOVE 1 TO SPACE-CONTROL.
*
        330-SEARCH-BRANCH-TABLE.
*
            SET BT-INDEX TO 1.
            SEARCH BT-ENTRIES
                AT END
                    MOVE "BRANCH NOT FOUND" TO BRANCH-NAME
                WHEN BT-BRANCH-NUMBER (BT-INDEX) = CM-BRANCH-NUMBER
                    MOVE BT-BRANCH-NAME (BT-INDEX) TO BRANCH-NAME
                WHEN BT-INDEX > BT-ENTRY-COUNT
                    MOVE "BRANCH NOT FOUND" TO BRANCH-NAME.
*
        340-PRINT-HEADING-LINES.
*
            ADD 1                 TO PAGE-COUNT.
            MOVE PAGE-COUNT       TO HDG1-PAGE-NUMBER.
            MOVE HEADING-LINE-1 TO PRINT-AREA.
            PERFORM 350-WRITE-PAGE-TOP-LINE.
            MOVE HEADING-LINE-2 TO PRINT-AREA.
            MOVE 1                TO SPACE-CONTROL.
            PERFORM 360-WRITE-REPORT-LINE.
            MOVE HEADING-LINE-3 TO PRINT-AREA.
            PERFORM 360-WRITE-REPORT-LINE.
            MOVE HEADING-LINE-4 TO PRINT-AREA.
            MOVE 2                TO SPACE-CONTROL.
            PERFORM 360-WRITE-REPORT-LINE.
            MOVE HEADING-LINE-5 TO PRINT-AREA.
            MOVE 1                TO SPACE-CONTROL.
            PERFORM 360-WRITE-REPORT-LINE.
            MOVE 2                TO SPACE-CONTROL.
*
        350-WRITE-PAGE-TOP-LINE.
*
            WRITE PRINT-AREA
                AFTER ADVANCING PAGE.
            MOVE 1 TO LINE-COUNT.
*
        360-WRITE-REPORT-LINE.
*
            WRITE PRINT-AREA
                AFTER ADVANCING SPACE-CONTROL LINES.
            ADD SPACE-CONTROL TO LINE-COUNT.
*
        370-ACCUMULATE-SALES-TOTALS.
*
            ADD CM-SALES-THIS-YTD TO BRANCH-TOTAL-THIS-YTD.
            ADD CM-SALES-LAST-YTD TO BRANCH-TOTAL-LAST-YTD.
            ADD CM-SALES-THIS-YTD TO GRAND-TOTAL-THIS-YTD.
            ADD CM-SALES-LAST-YTD TO GRAND-TOTAL-LAST-YTD.
```

```
*
 380-PRINT-BRANCH-LINE.
*
     MOVE BRANCH-TOTAL-THIS-YTD TO BL-SALES-THIS-YTD.
     MOVE BRANCH-TOTAL-LAST-YTD TO BL-SALES-LAST-YTD.
     COMPUTE CHANGE-AMOUNT =
         BRANCH-TOTAL-THIS-YTD - BRANCH-TOTAL-LAST-YTD.
     MOVE CHANGE-AMOUNT TO BL-CHANGE-AMOUNT.
     IF BRANCH-TOTAL-LAST-YTD NOT EQUAL ZERO
         COMPUTE BL-CHANGE-PERCENT ROUNDED =
             CHANGE-AMOUNT / BRANCH-TOTAL-LAST-YTD * 100
             ON SIZE ERROR
                 MOVE "OVRFLW" TO BL-CHANGE-PERCENT-R
         END-COMPUTE
     ELSE
         MOVE "  N/A"              TO BL-CHANGE-PERCENT-R.
     MOVE BRANCH-LINE TO PRINT-AREA.
     MOVE 2 TO SPACE-CONTROL.
     PERFORM 360-WRITE-REPORT-LINE.
     MOVE ZERO TO BRANCH-TOTAL-THIS-YTD
                  BRANCH-TOTAL-LAST-YTD.
*
 500-PRINT-GRAND-TOTALS.
*
     MOVE GRAND-TOTAL-THIS-YTD TO GTL-SALES-THIS-YTD.
     MOVE GRAND-TOTAL-LAST-YTD TO GTL-SALES-LAST-YTD.
     COMPUTE CHANGE-AMOUNT =
         GRAND-TOTAL-THIS-YTD - GRAND-TOTAL-LAST-YTD.
     MOVE CHANGE-AMOUNT TO GTL-CHANGE-AMOUNT.
     IF GRAND-TOTAL-LAST-YTD NOT EQUAL ZERO
         COMPUTE GTL-CHANGE-PERCENT ROUNDED =
             CHANGE-AMOUNT / GRAND-TOTAL-LAST-YTD * 100
             ON SIZE ERROR
                 MOVE "OVRFLW" TO GTL-CHANGE-PERCENT-R
         END-COMPUTE
     ELSE
         MOVE "  N/A"              TO GTL-CHANGE-PERCENT-R.
     MOVE GRAND-TOTAL-LINE TO PRINT-AREA.
     PERFORM 360-WRITE-REPORT-LINE.
```

Program 2

A batch update program

This model program uses the data in a sequential file of receipt transactions to update the records in an inventory master file. This master file is an indexed file with the item number field as the key. The basic logic of this program is to read a transaction record, read the master record that has the same item number on a random basis, update the fields in the master record, and rewrite the master record back on the disk.

In any update program, though, you want to make sure that the data in a transaction is valid before you use it to update the master record. As a result, much of this program has to do with editing the transaction records to make sure the data is valid and printing the invalid transactions so they can be corrected.

When a master file has indexed organization, its records can be read in sequence or in random order. In this program, random processing is used on the assumption that only a low percentage of the master records is going to be updated (low activity). If a high percentage is going to be updated, though, sequential processing is likely to be more efficient than random processing. In that case, the transaction records have to be in the same sequence as the master records.

Program specifications

Program name	INV2300		Page	1
Program description	Update inventory file		Date	11/20/96

Input/output specifications

File name	Description	Format	Use
RCPTTRAN	Receipt transaction file	Sequential	Input
INVMAST	Inventory master file	Indexed	Update
VRCPTRAN	Valid receipt transaction file	Sequential	Output
IRCPTLST	Invalid transaction listing	Print file	Output

Processing specifications

- The records in the receipt transaction file represent additions to inventory. These records are in sequence by item number, and they should be used to update the related records in the inventory master file.

- The records in the master file are indexed by item number (the key). Because the file processing activity is going to be low, the records should be read and updated on a random basis.

- Each record in the receipt transaction file must be edited before it is used for updating to make sure that all its fields are valid.

- If one or more fields in a receipt record are invalid, the record should be listed on the invalid transaction listing and the invalid field or fields should be preceded by an asterisk on the listing.

- If all the fields in a receipt record are valid, the record should be used to update the related fields in the inventory master record that has the same item number (key). Each valid record should also be written on the valid receipt transaction file for use by other programs. The valid records should have the same format and data as the input transaction records.

- The control totals for the update run should be printed on a separate page after the listing of the invalid receipt transactions.

Editing rules

Field name	Rules
RT-ITEM-NUMBER	Inventory master record must have same item number.
RT-VENDOR-NUMBER	Numeric and greater than zero.
RT-RECEIPT-DATE	The month, day, and year values in the form MM/DD/YY must be within valid ranges.
RT-RECEIPT-QUANTITY	Greater than zero.

COPY members

RCPTTRAN

```
01    RECEIPT-TRANSACTION.
*
      05    RT-ITEM-NUMBER              PIC X(5).
      05    RT-VENDOR-NUMBER            PIC X(4).
      05    RT-RECEIPT-DATE             PIC X(6).
      05    RT-RECEIPT-DATE-X           REDEFINES RT-RECEIPT-DATE.
            10    RT-RECEIPT-MONTH      PIC 99.
            10    RT-RECEIPT-DAY        PIC 99.
            10    RT-RECEIPT-YEAR       PIC 99.
      05    RT-RECEIPT-QUANTITY         PIC S9(5).
```

INVMAST

```
01    INVENTORY-MASTER-RECORD.
*
      05    IM-ITEM-NUMBER              PIC X(5).
      05    IM-ITEM-DESCRIPTION         PIC X(20).
      05    IM-UNIT-COST                PIC S9(3)V99.
      05    IM-UNIT-PRICE               PIC S9(3)V99.
      05    IM-ON-HAND-BALANCE          PIC S9(5).
      05    IM-UNIT-SALES-THIS-MONTH    PIC S9(5).
      05    IM-UNIT-SALES-THIS-YEAR     PIC S9(5).
      05    IM-UNIT-RECEIPTS-THIS-MONTH PIC S9(5).
      05    IM-UNIT-RECEIPTS-THIS-YEAR  PIC S9(5).
```

Notes

- The record layouts are intentionally simplified so the emphasis is on the structure and logic of the program, not on data manipulation. In actual practice, both of the records used in this program would contain many more fields.

- In actual practice, the definitions for the numeric fields in the disk records would probably include COMP-3 or PACKED-DECIMAL usage.

Subprograms

GETDATE

This subprogram gets the current date and time. To use it, you must pass a 10-character date and an 8-character time field to it. The date and time are returned in a format that's ready for use in the heading of a report.

DATEDIT

This subprogram edits a date field. To use it, you must pass a 6-character date field (MMDDYY) and a one-character switch field. This subprogram edits the date and sets the switch field to "N" if the field is invalid or "Y" if the field is valid.

Sample report

```
DATE:   02/12/1997        MIKE MURACH & ASSOCIATES, INC.          PAGE:     1
TIME:   03:44 PM                                                  INV2300
                                INVALID RECEIPT LISTING

   ITEM        VENDOR        DATE
  NUMBER       NUMBER      RECEIVED      QUANTITY

  *10000        1234       02/12/97         1000

   12345       *222A       02/12/97          100

   12345        3333      *02/29/97     *      0

  *22223        4444       02/12/97          100

   33333       *0000       02/12/97          100

  *44445        3456       02/12/97          100
```

```
DATE:   01/25/19          MIKE MURACH & ASSOCIATES, INC.          PAGE:     2
TIME:   01:44 PM                                                  INV2300


SUMMARY FOR INVENTORY RECEIPT RUN

     12 TRANSACTIONS READ
      6 VALID TRANSACTIONS
      6 INVALID TRANSACTIONS
```

Notes

- A sample report is given instead of a report layout so you can see what the printed output is supposed to look like.

- The length of each print line in this report is only 80 characters, instead of the normal 132, so the report can fit vertically on the page in this book.

The structure chart

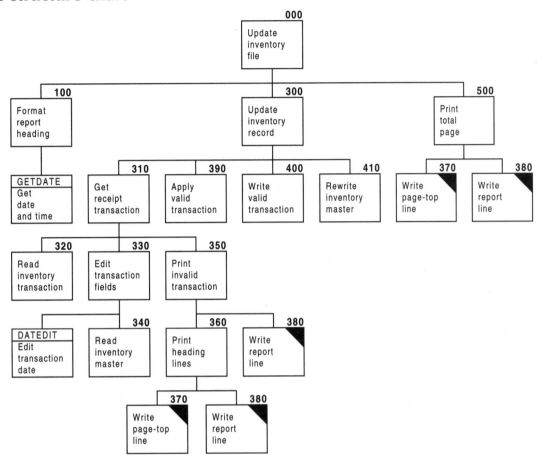

Notes

- The extended meaning of the *get* verb in module 310 is to read a transaction record, edit it, and print a line on the invalid transaction listing if the record is invalid.

- Module 330 calls whatever subprograms or other modules it needs to edit the fields in a transaction record. To edit the item number field, it calls module 340 to see whether a master record with the same key is in the file.

Source listing notes

Compiler used

- This program was compiled and tested using the Micro Focus Workbench with the VS COBOL II Version 4.0 compiler options.

Working-Storage Section

- The LINE-COUNT and LINES-ON-PAGE fields are used by module 350 to determine whether or not the page is full and heading lines need to be printed on the next page. These fields are initialized with values that cause the headings to be printed on the first page of the report.

- In this program and in model program 1, the first three heading lines are defined so the report number and report title can be moved into these heading lines in the format-report-heading module. When you define the heading lines this way, you can create a COPY member for them that is used by all programs that prepare reports. This helps standardize the format of the report headings.

300-UPDATE-INVENTORY-RECORD

- This simple module calls module 310 until it gets a valid transaction record or until there are no more records in the transaction file. When it gets a valid transaction, it calls modules 390, 400, and 410 to do the required update functions.

310-GET-RECEIPT-TRANSACTION

- This module calls module 320 to read a record, 330 to edit the record, and 350 to print a line on the invalid transaction listing if the record is invalid.

330-EDIT-TRANSACTION-FIELDS

- This module calls the DATEDIT subprogram to edit the date. It also calls module 340 to read an inventory master record that has the same item number as the transaction record. If that record can't be found, the item number field is invalid. Because this module moves an asterisk (*) before each field that's invalid, this module starts by moving spaces to the invalid-transaction line to clear the asterisks from the previous record.

Source listing

```
IDENTIFICATION DIVISION.
*
PROGRAM-ID.      INV2300.
*
ENVIRONMENT DIVISION.
*
CONFIGURATION SECTION.
*
INPUT-OUTPUT SECTION.
*
FILE-CONTROL.
    SELECT INVMAST  ASSIGN TO INVMAST
                    ORGANIZATION IS INDEXED
                    ACCESS IS RANDOM
                    RECORD KEY IS IR-ITEM-NUMBER.
    SELECT RCPTTRAN ASSIGN TO RCPTTRAN.
    SELECT VRCPTRAN ASSIGN TO VRCPTRAN.
    SELECT IRCPTLST ASSIGN TO IRCPTLST.
*
DATA DIVISION.
*
FILE SECTION.
*
FD  RCPTTRAN
    LABEL RECORDS ARE STANDARD
    RECORD CONTAINS 20 CHARACTERS.
*
01  TRANSACTION-RECORD          PIC X(20).
*
FD  INVMAST
    LABEL RECORDS ARE STANDARD
    RECORD CONTAINS 60 CHARACTERS.
*
01  INVENTORY-RECORD.
*
    05  IR-ITEM-NUMBER          PIC X(5).
    05  FILLER                  PIC X(55).
*
FD  VRCPTRAN
    LABEL RECORDS ARE STANDARD
    RECORD CONTAINS 20 CHARACTERS.
*
01  VALID-RECEIPT-TRANSACTION   PIC X(20).
*
FD  IRCPTLST
    LABEL RECORDS ARE STANDARD
    RECORD CONTAINS 132 CHARACTERS.
*
01  PRINT-AREA                  PIC X(132).
*
```

```
WORKING-STORAGE SECTION.
*
01  SWITCHES.
*
    05  RCPTTRAN-EOF-SWITCH        PIC X         VALUE "N".
        88  RCPTTRAN-EOF                         VALUE "Y".
    05  VALID-TRAN-SWITCH          PIC X.
        88  VALID-TRAN                           VALUE "Y".
    05  VALID-DATE-SWITCH          PIC X.
        88  VALID-DATE                           VALUE "Y".
    05  MASTER-FOUND-SWITCH        PIC X.
        88  MASTER-FOUND                         VALUE "Y".
*
01  PRINT-FIELDS               PACKED-DECIMAL.
*
    05  LINE-COUNT             PIC S999      VALUE +999.
    05  LINES-ON-PAGE          PIC S999      VALUE +57.
    05  SPACE-CONTROL          PIC S9.
    05  PAGE-COUNT             PIC S999      VALUE ZERO.
*
01  DATE-AND-TIME-FIELDS.
*
    05  TODAYS-DATE            PIC X(10).
    05  TODAYS-TIME            PIC X(8).
*
01  COUNT-FIELDS              PACKED-DECIMAL.
*
    05  TRANSACTION-COUNT      PIC S9(5)     VALUE ZERO.
    05  VALID-COUNT            PIC S9(5)     VALUE ZERO.
    05  INVALID-COUNT          PIC S9(5)     VALUE ZERO.
*
COPY RCPTTRAN.
*
COPY INVMAST.
*
01  REPORT-TITLE.
*
    05  FILLER       PIC X(9)    VALUE SPACE.
    05  FILLER       PIC X(24)   VALUE "INVALID RECEIPT REGISTER".
    05  FILLER       PIC X(7)    VALUE SPACE.
*
01  HEADING-LINE-1.
*
    05  FILLER              PIC X(7)     VALUE "DATE:".
    05  HDG1-DATE           PIC X(10).
    05  FILLER              PIC X(8)     VALUE SPACE.
    05  FILLER              PIC X(15)    VALUE "MIKE MURACH & A".
    05  FILLER              PIC X(15)    VALUE "SSOCIATES, INC.".
    05  FILLER              PIC X(15)    VALUE SPACE.
    05  FILLER              PIC X(6)     VALUE "PAGE:".
    05  HDG1-PAGE-NUMBER    PIC ZZZ9.
    05  FILLER              PIC X(52)    VALUE SPACE.
*
01  HEADING-LINE-2.
*
    05  FILLER              PIC X(7)     VALUE "TIME:".
    05  HDG2-TIME           PIC X(8).
    05  FILLER              PIC X(55)    VALUE SPACE.
    05  HDG2-REPORT-NUMBER  PIC X(10).
    05  FILLER              PIC X(52)    VALUE SPACE.
```

```
*
 01   HEADING-LINE-3.
*
     05   FILLER                PIC X(20)    VALUE SPACE.
     05   HDG3-REPORT-TITLE     PIC X(40).
     05   FILLER                PIC X(72)    VALUE SPACE.
*
 01   HEADING-LINE-4.
*
     05   FILLER            PIC X(20)    VALUE " ITEM        VENDOR    ".
     05   FILLER            PIC X(20)    VALUE "   DATE                ".
     05   FILLER            PIC X(92)    VALUE SPACE.
*
 01   HEADING-LINE-5.
*
     05   FILLER            PIC X(20)    VALUE "NUMBER      NUMBER   ".
     05   FILLER            PIC X(20)    VALUE " RECEIVED    QUANTI".
     05   FILLER            PIC X(20)    VALUE "TY                  ".
     05   FILLER            PIC X(72)    VALUE SPACE.
*
 01   INVALID-TRANSACTION-LINE.
*
     05   ITL-ITEM-NUMBER-ERR PIC X.
     05   ITL-ITEM-NUMBER     PIC X(5).
     05   FILLER              PIC X(5)     VALUE SPACE.
     05   ITL-VENDOR-NUMBER-ERR PIC X.
     05   ITL-VENDOR-NUMBER   PIC X(4).
     05   FILLER              PIC X(5)     VALUE SPACE.
     05   ITL-DATE-ERR        PIC X.
     05   ITL-DATE            PIC XX/XX/XX.
     05   FILLER              PIC X(5)     VALUE SPACE.
     05   ITL-RECEIPT-QTY-ERR PIC X.
     05   ITL-RECEIPT-QTY     PIC ZZZZ9.
     05   FILLER              PIC X(91)    VALUE SPACE.
*
 01   TOTAL-LINE-1.
*
     05   FILLER            PIC X(20)    VALUE "SUMMARY FOR INVENTOR".
     05   FILLER            PIC X(20)    VALUE "Y RECEIPT RUN       ".
     05   FILLER            PIC X(92)    VALUE SPACE.
*
 01   TOTAL-LINE-2.
*
     05   TOT2-TRAN-COUNT PIC ZZ,ZZ9.
     05   FILLER            PIC X(20)    VALUE " TRANSACTIONS READ  ".
     05   FILLER            PIC X(106)   VALUE SPACES.
*
 01   TOTAL-LINE-3.
*
     05   TOT3-VAL-COUNT  PIC ZZ,ZZ9.
     05   FILLER            PIC X(20)    VALUE " VALID TRANSACTIONS ".
     05   FILLER            PIC X(106)   VALUE SPACES.
*
 01   TOTAL-LINE-4.
*
     05   TOT4-INV-COUNT  PIC ZZ,ZZ9.
     05   FILLER            PIC X(20)    VALUE " INVALID TRANSACTION".
     05   FILLER            PIC X(20)    VALUE "S                   ".
     05   FILLER            PIC X(86)    VALUE SPACES.
```

```
*
 PROCEDURE DIVISION.
*
 000-UPDATE-INVENTORY-FILE.
*
     OPEN INPUT   RCPTTRAN
          I-O     INVMAST
          OUTPUT  VRCPTRAN
                  IRCPTLST.
     PERFORM 100-FORMAT-REPORT-HEADING.
     PERFORM 300-UPDATE-INVENTORY-RECORD
         UNTIL RCPTTRAN-EOF.
     PERFORM 500-PRINT-TOTAL-PAGE.
     CLOSE RCPTTRAN
           INVMAST
           VRCPTRAN
           IRCPTLST.
     STOP RUN.
*
 100-FORMAT-REPORT-HEADING.
*
     CALL "GETDATE" USING TODAYS-DATE TODAYS-TIME.
     MOVE TODAYS-DATE TO HDG1-DATE.
     MOVE TODAYS-TIME TO HDG2-TIME.
     MOVE "INV2300"     TO HDG2-REPORT-NUMBER.
     MOVE REPORT-TITLE TO HDG3-REPORT-TITLE.
*
 300-UPDATE-INVENTORY-RECORD.
*
     MOVE "N" TO VALID-TRAN-SWITCH.
     PERFORM 310-GET-RECEIPT-TRANSACTION
         UNTIL VALID-TRAN
             OR RCPTTRAN-EOF.
     IF NOT RCPTTRAN-EOF
         PERFORM 390-APPLY-VALID-TRANSACTION
         PERFORM 400-WRITE-VALID-TRANSACTION
         PERFORM 410-REWRITE-INVENTORY-MASTER.
*
 310-GET-RECEIPT-TRANSACTION.
*
     MOVE "Y" TO VALID-TRAN-SWITCH.
     PERFORM 320-READ-INVENTORY-TRANSACTION.
     IF NOT RCPTTRAN-EOF
         ADD 1 TO TRANSACTION-COUNT
         PERFORM 330-EDIT-TRANSACTION-FIELDS
         IF NOT VALID-TRAN
             PERFORM 350-PRINT-INVALID-TRANSACTION.
*
 320-READ-INVENTORY-TRANSACTION.
*
     READ RCPTTRAN INTO RECEIPT-TRANSACTION
         AT END
             MOVE "Y" TO RCPTTRAN-EOF-SWITCH.
```

```
*
 330-EDIT-TRANSACTION-FIELDS.
*
     MOVE SPACE TO INVALID-TRANSACTION-LINE.
     MOVE RT-ITEM-NUMBER TO IR-ITEM-NUMBER.
     MOVE "Y" TO MASTER-FOUND-SWITCH.
     PERFORM 340-READ-INVENTORY-MASTER.
     IF NOT MASTER-FOUND
         MOVE "*" TO ITL-ITEM-NUMBER-ERR
         MOVE "N" TO VALID-TRAN-SWITCH.
     IF   RT-VENDOR-NUMBER NOT NUMERIC
       OR RT-VENDOR-NUMBER NOT GREATER THAN ZERO
         MOVE "*" TO ITL-VENDOR-NUMBER-ERR
         MOVE "N" TO VALID-TRAN-SWITCH.
     CALL "DATEDIT" USING RT-RECEIPT-DATE VALID-DATE-SWITCH.
     IF NOT VALID-DATE
         MOVE "*" TO ITL-DATE-ERR
         MOVE "N" TO VALID-TRAN-SWITCH.
     IF RT-RECEIPT-QUANTITY NOT GREATER THAN ZERO
         MOVE "*" TO ITL-RECEIPT-QTY-ERR
         MOVE "N" TO VALID-TRAN-SWITCH.
*
 340-READ-INVENTORY-MASTER.
*
     READ INVMAST INTO INVENTORY-MASTER-RECORD
         INVALID KEY
             MOVE "N" TO MASTER-FOUND-SWITCH.
*
 350-PRINT-INVALID-TRANSACTION.
*
     IF LINE-COUNT GREATER THAN LINES-ON-PAGE
         PERFORM 360-PRINT-HEADING-LINES.
     MOVE RT-ITEM-NUMBER            TO ITL-ITEM-NUMBER.
     MOVE RT-VENDOR-NUMBER          TO ITL-VENDOR-NUMBER.
     MOVE RT-RECEIPT-DATE           TO ITL-DATE.
     MOVE RT-RECEIPT-QUANTITY       TO ITL-RECEIPT-QTY.
     MOVE INVALID-TRANSACTION-LINE TO PRINT-AREA.
     PERFORM 380-WRITE-REPORT-LINE.
     ADD 1 TO INVALID-COUNT.
*
 360-PRINT-HEADING-LINES.
*
     ADD 1                 TO PAGE-COUNT.
     MOVE PAGE-COUNT       TO HDG1-PAGE-NUMBER.
     MOVE HEADING-LINE-1 TO PRINT-AREA.
     PERFORM 370-WRITE-PAGE-TOP-LINE.
     MOVE HEADING-LINE-2 TO PRINT-AREA.
     MOVE 1                 TO SPACE-CONTROL.
     PERFORM 380-WRITE-REPORT-LINE.
     MOVE HEADING-LINE-3 TO PRINT-AREA.
     PERFORM 380-WRITE-REPORT-LINE.
     MOVE HEADING-LINE-4 TO PRINT-AREA.
     MOVE 2                 TO SPACE-CONTROL.
     PERFORM 380-WRITE-REPORT-LINE.
     MOVE HEADING-LINE-5 TO PRINT-AREA.
     MOVE 1                 TO SPACE-CONTROL.
     PERFORM 380-WRITE-REPORT-LINE.
     MOVE 2                 TO SPACE-CONTROL.
```

```
*
 370-WRITE-PAGE-TOP-LINE.
*
     WRITE PRINT-AREA
         AFTER ADVANCING PAGE.
     MOVE 1 TO LINE-COUNT.
*
 380-WRITE-REPORT-LINE.
*
     WRITE PRINT-AREA
         AFTER ADVANCING SPACE-CONTROL LINES.
     ADD SPACE-CONTROL TO LINE-COUNT.
*
 390-APPLY-VALID-TRANSACTION.
*
     ADD RT-RECEIPT-QUANTITY TO IM-ON-HAND-BALANCE.
*
 400-WRITE-VALID-TRANSACTION.
*
     WRITE VALID-RECEIPT-TRANSACTION FROM RECEIPT-TRANSACTION.
     ADD 1 TO VALID-COUNT.
*
 410-REWRITE-INVENTORY-MASTER.
*
     REWRITE INVENTORY-RECORD FROM INVENTORY-MASTER-RECORD.
*
 500-PRINT-TOTAL-PAGE.
*
     ADD 1                  TO PAGE-COUNT.
     MOVE PAGE-COUNT        TO HDG1-PAGE-NUMBER.
     MOVE HEADING-LINE-1    TO PRINT-AREA.
     PERFORM 370-WRITE-PAGE-TOP-LINE.
     MOVE HEADING-LINE-2    TO PRINT-AREA.
     MOVE 1                 TO SPACE-CONTROL.
     PERFORM 380-WRITE-REPORT-LINE.
     MOVE TOTAL-LINE-1      TO PRINT-AREA.
     MOVE 3                 TO SPACE-CONTROL.
     PERFORM 380-WRITE-REPORT-LINE.
     MOVE TRANSACTION-COUNT TO TOT2-TRAN-COUNT.
     MOVE TOTAL-LINE-2      TO PRINT-AREA.
     MOVE 2                 TO SPACE-CONTROL.
     PERFORM 380-WRITE-REPORT-LINE.
     MOVE VALID-COUNT       TO TOT3-VAL-COUNT.
     MOVE TOTAL-LINE-3      TO PRINT-AREA.
     MOVE 1                 TO SPACE-CONTROL.
     PERFORM 380-WRITE-REPORT-LINE.
     MOVE INVALID-COUNT     TO TOT4-INV-COUNT.
     MOVE TOTAL-LINE-4      TO PRINT-AREA.
     PERFORM 380-WRITE-REPORT-LINE.
```

Program 3

An interactive program in Micro Focus COBOL

This model program is used to add, delete, or change records in a customer master file. It gets the data that it needs for this maintenance directly from the computer user who is working at a PC or workstation. Before the data is used to maintain a record, though, it is edited for completeness and validity.

This program is written in Micro Focus COBOL with each screen defined in the Screen Section of the Data Division. Then, each DISPLAY statement displays an entire screen and each ACCEPT statement accepts all the input fields in an entire screen. This is typical of the way most interactive programs in production environments are written.

Although the Micro Focus COBOL options can be varied in many ways to meet the requirements of the user, the intent of this model program is to show the structure and coding logic for a program like this, not the coding details and variations. As a result, this program uses the COBOL options that lead to the code that's easiest to read and understand. No matter what options you use, though, you can use the same structure and similar coding logic.

Program specifications

Program name	CUSTMNT1	Page	1
Program description	Maintain customer file	Date	11/20/96

Input/output specifications

File name	Description	Format	Use
CUSTMAST	Customer master file	Indexed	I-O
SCREEN1	Customer key screen	Screen	I-O
SCREEN2	Customer data screen	Screen	I-O

Processing specifications

- When the key screen is displayed, the user enters a customer key and an action code. If the user selects Add, the customer key must *not* be in the master file. If the user selects Change or Delete, the customer key must be in the master file.

- If the user enters a valid combination of customer key and action, the program displays the data screen. For an Add, the user enters the new customer information on this screen. For a Change, the user modifies the necessary fields that are displayed. For a Deletion, the user confirms that this is the record that should be deleted.

- If the user presses F3 at either the key screen or the maintenance screen, the program should end and return to the menu program that started it.

- If the user presses F10 from the key screen, the entries should be cleared and the key screen should be displayed again so the user can start the entries over. If the user presses F10 from the data screen, the program should return to the key screen without processing any of the data that was entered.

Editing rules

Field name	Rules
CM-CUSTOMER-NUMBER	Required numeric entry.
CM-LAST-NAME	Required entry.
CM-FIRST-NAME	Required entry.
CM-ADDRESS	Required entry.
CM-CITY	Required entry.
CM-STATE	Required entry. Must be a valid USPS state code (use the subprogram named STATEDIT to check the validity).
CM-ZIP-CODE	Required entry. Must be a valid USPS zip code for the related state code (use the subprogram named ZIPEDIT to check the validity).

COPY member

CUSTMAST

```
01  CUSTOMER-MASTER-RECORD.
*
    05  CM-CUSTOMER-NUMBER     PIC  X(6).
    05  CM-LAST-NAME           PIC  X(30).
    05  CM-FIRST-NAME          PIC  X(20).
    05  CM-ADDRESS             PIC  X(30).
    05  CM-CITY                PIC  X(20).
    05  CM-STATE               PIC  X(2).
    05  CM-ZIP-CODE            PIC  X(9).
```

Subprograms

STATEDIT

This subprogram edits a state code for validity. To use it, you must pass a two-character state code and a one-character switch. If the state code is valid, the subprogram returns a value of "Y" in the switch field. If the field is invalid, the subprogram returns a value of "N."

ZIPEDIT

This subprogram edits the first five digits of a nine-digit zip code. To use it, you must pass a two-character state code, a nine-character zip code, and a one-character switch. If the first five digits of the zip code are valid, the subprogram returns a value of "Y" in the switch field. If the first five digits are invalid, the subprogram returns a value of "N."

Screen layouts

Key screen

```
          1         2         3         4         5         6         7         8
 12345678901234567890123456789012345678901234567890123456789012345678901234567890
  ┌─────────────────────────────────────────────────────────────────────────────┐
 1│ Customer Maintenance                                      Date: 02/12/1997    │
 2│                                                                               │
 3│ Type a customer number.  Then select an action and press Enter.               │
 4│                                                                               │
 5│ Customer number. . . . . XXXXXX                                               │
 6│                                                                               │
 7│ Action . . . . . . . . . X 1.   Add a new customer                            │
 8│                            2.   Change an existing customer                   │
 9│                            3.   Delete an existing customer                   │
10│                                                                               │
11│                                                                               │
12│                                                                               │
13│                                                                               │
14│                                                                               │
15│                                                                               │
16│                                                                               │
17│                                                                               │
18│                                                                               │
19│                                                                               │
20│                                                                               │
21│                                                                               │
22│                                                                               │
23│ XXXXXXXXXXXXXXXXXXXXXXXXXXXXXXXXXXXXXXXXXXXXXXXXXXXXXXXXXXXXXXXXXXXXXXXXXXXXXX  │
24│ F3=Exit    F10=Cancel                                                         │
  └─────────────────────────────────────────────────────────────────────────────┘
```

Data screen

```
          1         2         3         4         5         6         7         8
 12345678901234567890123456789012345678901234567890123456789012345678901234567890
  ┌─────────────────────────────────────────────────────────────────────────────┐
 1│ Customer Maintenance                                      Date: 02/12/1997    │
 2│                                                                               │
 3│ XXXXXXXXXXXXXXXXXXXXXXXXXXXXXXXXXXXXXXXXXXXXXXXXXXXXXXXXXXXXXXXXXXXXXXXXXXXXXX  │
 4│                                                                               │
 5│ Customer number. . . . . XXXXXX                                               │
 6│                                                                               │
 7│ Last name. . . . . . .   XXXXXXXXXXXXXXXXXXXXXXXXXXXXXX                        │
 8│ First name . . . . . .   XXXXXXXXXXXXXXXXXXXX                                  │
 9│ Address. . . . . . . .   XXXXXXXXXXXXXXXXXXXXXXXXXXXXXX                        │
10│ City . . . . . . . . .   XXXXXXXXXXXXXXXXXXXX                                  │
11│ State. . . . . . . . .   XX                                                   │
12│ Zip code . . . . . . .   XXXXXXXXX                                            │
13│                                                                               │
14│                                                                               │
15│                                                                               │
16│                                                                               │
17│                                                                               │
18│                                                                               │
19│                                                                               │
20│                                                                               │
21│                                                                               │
22│                                                                               │
23│ XXXXXXXXXXXXXXXXXXXXXXXXXXXXXXXXXXXXXXXXXXXXXXXXXXXXXXXXXXXXXXXXXXXXXXXXXXXXXX  │
24│ F3=Exit    F10=Cancel                                                         │
  └─────────────────────────────────────────────────────────────────────────────┘
```

Event/Response chart

Program name	CUSTMNT1		Page	1
Program description	Maintain customer file		Date	11/20/96

Event/response summary

Event	Context	Response	New context
Program start	N/A	Display the key screen.	Get key
F3	All	Return to the calling program.	N/A
F10	Get key	Clear entries and display the key screen again.	Get key
	Add customer Change customer Delete customer	Cancel operation and display the key screen.	Get key
Enter	Get key	Edit the input data. If valid display the data screen	Add customer, Change customer, or Delete customer
		Else display an error message.	Get key
	Add customer	Edit the input data. If valid add the customer record display the key screen Else	Get key
		display an error message.	Add customer
	Change customer	Edit the input data. If valid change customer record display the key screen Else	Get key
		display an error message.	Change customer
	Delete customer	If verified delete customer record. Display the key screen.	Get key
Other key	All	Display an error message.	Unchanged

The structure chart

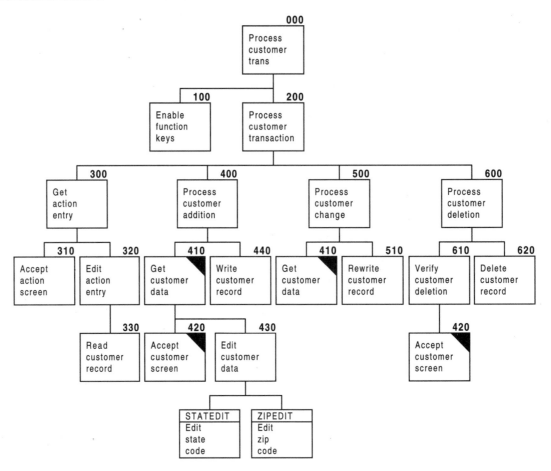

Notes

- Module 100 just calls a subprogram to enable the use of function keys 1 through 10. This type of setup module is typical in an interactive program.

- Module 300 illustrates the use of the *get* verb in an interactive program. It means to accept the data from a screen and edit that data.

- Module 410 is a common module that is used to *get* the customer data for an addition or a change. It calls module 430 to edit this data since added records and changed records have the same editing requirements.

Source listing notes

Working-Storage Section

- The ENABLE-FUNCTION-KEY-FIELDS are required by the subprogram that enables the use of the function keys. Once enabled, the KEY-STATUS condition names identify the key that was pressed at the last ACCEPT screen.

- The ATTRIBUTE-CONTROL-FIELDS can be used to dynamically assign an attribute to a field on the screen. If, for example, you move the HIGHLIGHT attribute to one of these control fields, the related field in the Screen Section is highlighted when next displayed.

- The Screen Section is used to define the two screens used by this program and the constants and variables that apply to those screens.

200-PROCESS-CUSTOMER-TRAN

- This module performs module 300 until it gets a valid action screen (a valid combination of customer number and action code) or until the user presses F3 or F10. Then, if the action screen is valid, this module calls module 400, 500, or 600 to process the maintenance request.

300-GET-ACTION-ENTRY

- This module performs module 310 to accept the action screen. Then, if the user presses the Enter key to complete the screen, this module calls module 320 to edit the customer number and action code. Otherwise, it sets the proper switch for whichever function key was pressed.

320-EDIT-ACTION-ENTRY

- This is typical of an interactive edit module. It edits the fields in the reverse order of the way they appear on the screen. That way, the error message in line 23 applies to the first error field on the screen and the cursor is at the start of that field.

400-PROCESS-CUSTOMER-ADDITION and
500-PROCESS-CUSTOMER-CHANGE

- These modules are similar to module 200 in that they call module 410 until the data on the customer screen is valid. Module 410 in turn is similar to module 300. And module 600 is similar to modules 400 and 500. Similarities like these make it easier to code, debug, and maintain a program.

430-EDIT-CUSTOMER-DATA

- This module is similar to module 320, the other edit module. It edits the fields in the reverse order of the way they appear on the customer data screen. For each invalid field, a message is moved to line 23, the cursor is moved to the start of the field, and the HIGHLIGHT attribute is applied to the field (if the field isn't blank).

Source listing

```
     IDENTIFICATION DIVISION.
*
     PROGRAM-ID.      CUSTMNT1.
*
     ENVIRONMENT DIVISION.
*
     CONFIGURATION SECTION.
*
     SPECIAL-NAMES.
*
         CONSOLE IS CRT
         CRT STATUS IS KEY-STATUS
         CURSOR IS CURSOR-POSITION.
*
     INPUT-OUTPUT SECTION.
*
     FILE-CONTROL.
*
         SELECT CUSTMAST ASSIGN TO "c:\cobolmf\custmstm.dat"
                         ORGANIZATION IS INDEXED
                         ACCESS IS RANDOM
                         RECORD KEY IS CM-KEY.
*
     DATA DIVISION.
*
     FILE SECTION.
*
     FD   CUSTMAST
          LABEL RECORDS ARE STANDARD.
*
     01   CM-RECORD.
*
          05   CM-KEY       PIC X(6).
          05   FILLER       PIC X(111).
*
     WORKING-STORAGE SECTION.
*
     01   CURSOR-POSITION.
*
          05   CURSOR-ROW               PIC 99.
          05   CURSOR-COLUMN            PIC 99.
*
     01   ENABLE-FUNCTION-KEY-FIELDS.
*
          05   FLAG                     PIC 99      VALUE 1     COMP-X.
          05   USER-KEY-CONTROL.
               10   ENABLE-FN-KEYS      PIC 99      VALUE 1     COMP-X.
               10   FILLER              PIC X       VALUE "1".
               10   FIRST-USER-KEY      PIC 99      VALUE 1     COMP-X.
               10   NUMBER-OF-KEYS      PIC 99      VALUE 10    COMP-X.
*
     01   KEY-STATUS.
*
          05   TERMINATION-CONDITION-CODE  PIC 9.
               88   ENTER-KEY               VALUE 0.
               88   FUNCTION-KEY            VALUE 1.
          05   FUNCTION-KEY-CODE           PIC 99       COMP-X.
               88   F1                      VALUE 1.
               88   F2                      VALUE 2.
```

```
                    88   F3                   VALUE 3.
                    88   F4                   VALUE 4.
                    88   F5                   VALUE 5.
                    88   F6                   VALUE 6.
                    88   F7                   VALUE 7.
                    88   F8                   VALUE 8.
                    88   F9                   VALUE 9.
                    88   F10                  VALUE 10.
           05   FILLER                   PIC X.
  *
    01   SWITCHES.
  *
           05   END-PROGRAM-SW           PIC X    VALUE "N".
                88   END-PROGRAM              VALUE "Y".
           05   CANCEL-ENTRY-SW          PIC X    VALUE "N".
                88   CANCEL-ENTRY             VALUE "Y".
           05   RECORD-FOUND-SW          PIC X    VALUE "Y".
                88   RECORD-FOUND             VALUE "Y".
           05   VALID-ACTION-SW          PIC X    VALUE "N".
                88   VALID-ACTION             VALUE "Y".
           05   VALID-DATA-SW            PIC X    VALUE "N".
                88   VALID-DATA               VALUE "Y".
           05   VALID-STATE-SW           PIC X    VALUE "N".
                88   VALID-STATE              VALUE "Y".
           05   VALID-ZIP-CODE-SW        PIC X    VALUE "N".
                88   VALID-ZIP-CODE           VALUE "Y".
  *
    01   FLAGS.
  *
           05   ACTION-CODE              PIC X.
                88   CUSTOMER-ADDITION        VALUE "1".
                88   CUSTOMER-CHANGE          VALUE "2".
                88   CUSTOMER-DELETION        VALUE "3".
  *
    01   DATE-AND-TIME-FIELDS.
  *
           05   TODAYS-DATE              PIC X(10).
           05   TODAYS-TIME              PIC X(8).
  *
    COPY CUSTMAST.
  *
    01   SCREEN-HEADING-LINE.
  *
           05   SHL-PROGRAM-NAME         PIC X(50).
           05   FILLER                   PIC X(14)      VALUE SPACE.
           05   FILLER                   PIC X(6)       VALUE "Date: ".
           05   SHL-TODAYS-DATE          PIC X(10).
  *
    01   SCREEN-MESSAGE-LINES.
  *
           05   MESSAGE-LINE-3  PIC X(80) VALUE SPACE.
           05   MESSAGE-LINE-23 PIC X(80) VALUE SPACE.
           05   MESSAGE-LINE-24.
                10   FILLER      PIC X(10) VALUE "F3=Exit".
                10   FILLER      PIC X(10) VALUE "F10=Cancel".
                10   FILLER      PIC X(60) VALUE SPACE.
```

```
*
 01   ATTRIBUTE-CONTROL-FIELDS.

     05   CUST-NUMBER-CONTROL      PIC X(20).
     05   LAST-NAME-CONTROL        PIC X(20).
     05   FIRST-NAME-CONTROL       PIC X(20).
     05   ADDRESS-CONTROL          PIC X(20).
     05   CITY-CONTROL             PIC X(20).
     05   STATE-CONTROL            PIC X(20).
     05   ZIP-CODE-CONTROL         PIC X(20).
*
 SCREEN SECTION.
*
 01   ACTION-SCREEN.
*
     05   BLANK SCREEN.
     05   LINE 1  COLUMN 1 PIC X(80)  FROM SCREEN-HEADING-LINE.
     05   LINE 3  COLUMN 1  VALUE "Type a customer number. Then sel
-        "ect an action and press Enter.".
     05   LINE 5  COLUMN 1  VALUE "Customer number. . . . . ".
     05   LINE 5  COLUMN 26 PIC X(6)   USING CM-KEY
          CONTROL CUST-NUMBER-CONTROL  AUTO.
     05   LINE 7  COLUMN 1  VALUE "Action . . . . . . . . . ".
     05   LINE 7  COLUMN 26 PIC X       USING ACTION-CODE.
     05   LINE 7  COLUMN 28 VALUE "1. Add a new customer          ".
     05   LINE 8  COLUMN 28 VALUE "2. Change an existing customer".
     05   LINE 9  COLUMN 28 VALUE "3. Delete an existing customer".
     05   LINE 23 COLUMN 1  PIC X(80)  FROM MESSAGE-LINE-23
          HIGHLIGHT.
     05   LINE 24 COLUMN 1  PIC X(80)  FROM MESSAGE-LINE-24.
*
 01   CUSTOMER-DATA-SCREEN.
*
     05   BLANK SCREEN.
     05   LINE 1  COLUMN 1  PIC X(80)  FROM SCREEN-HEADING-LINE.
     05   LINE 3  COLUMN 1  PIC X(80)  FROM MESSAGE-LINE-3.
     05   LINE 5  COLUMN 1  VALUE "Customer number. . . . . ".
     05   LINE 5  COLUMN 26 PIC 9(6)    FROM CM-CUSTOMER-NUMBER.
     05   LINE 7  COLUMN 1  VALUE "Last name. . . . . . . . ".
     05   LINE 7  COLUMN 26 PIC X(30)  USING CM-LAST-NAME
          CONTROL LAST-NAME-CONTROL.
     05   LINE 8  COLUMN 1  VALUE "First name . . . . . . . ".
     05   LINE 8  COLUMN 26 PIC X(30)  USING CM-FIRST-NAME
          CONTROL FIRST-NAME-CONTROL.
     05   LINE 9  COLUMN 1  VALUE "Address. . . . . . . . . ".
     05   LINE 9  COLUMN 26 PIC X(30)  USING CM-ADDRESS
          CONTROL ADDRESS-CONTROL.
     05   LINE 10 COLUMN 1  VALUE "City . . . . . . . . . . ".
     05   LINE 10 COLUMN 26 PIC X(20)  USING CM-CITY
          CONTROL CITY-CONTROL.
     05   LINE 11 COLUMN 1  VALUE "State. . . . . . . . . . ".
     05   LINE 11 COLUMN 26 PIC XX      USING CM-STATE
          CONTROL STATE-CONTROL        AUTO.
     05   LINE 12 COLUMN 1  VALUE "Zip code . . . . . . . . ".
     05   LINE 12 COLUMN 26 PIC X(9)   USING CM-ZIP-CODE
          CONTROL ZIP-CODE-CONTROL     AUTO.
     05   LINE 23 COLUMN 1  PIC X(80)  FROM MESSAGE-LINE-23
          HIGHLIGHT.
     05   LINE 24 COLUMN 1  PIC X(80)  FROM MESSAGE-LINE-24.
```

```
*
 PROCEDURE DIVISION.
*
 000-PROCESS-CUSTOMER-TRANS.
*
     CALL "GETDATE" USING TODAYS-DATE TODAYS-TIME.
     MOVE TODAYS-DATE TO SHL-TODAYS-DATE.
     MOVE "Customer maintenance" TO SHL-PROGRAM-NAME.
     OPEN I-O CUSTMAST.
     PERFORM 100-ENABLE-FUNCTION-KEYS.
     PERFORM 200-PROCESS-CUSTOMER-TRAN
         UNTIL END-PROGRAM.
     CLOSE CUSTMAST.
     STOP RUN.
*
 100-ENABLE-FUNCTION-KEYS.
*
     CALL X"AF" USING FLAG USER-KEY-CONTROL.
*
 200-PROCESS-CUSTOMER-TRAN.
*
     MOVE SPACE   TO ACTION-CODE
                     CM-KEY
                     MESSAGE-LINE-23.
     MOVE 1       TO CURSOR-ROW
                     CURSOR-COLUMN.
     MOVE "N"     TO VALID-ACTION-SW
                     CANCEL-ENTRY-SW.
     PERFORM 300-GET-ACTION-ENTRY
         UNTIL VALID-ACTION
             OR CANCEL-ENTRY
             OR END-PROGRAM.
     IF VALID-ACTION
         IF CUSTOMER-ADDITION
             PERFORM 400-PROCESS-CUSTOMER-ADDITION
         ELSE IF CUSTOMER-CHANGE
             PERFORM 500-PROCESS-CUSTOMER-CHANGE
         ELSE IF CUSTOMER-DELETION
             PERFORM 600-PROCESS-CUSTOMER-DELETION.
*
 300-GET-ACTION-ENTRY.
*
     MOVE "Y" TO VALID-ACTION-SW.
     PERFORM 310-ACCEPT-ACTION-SCREEN.
     IF ENTER-KEY
         PERFORM 320-EDIT-ACTION-ENTRY.
     IF FUNCTION-KEY
         MOVE "N" TO VALID-ACTION-SW
         EVALUATE FUNCTION-KEY-CODE
             WHEN 3
                 MOVE "Y" TO END-PROGRAM-SW
             WHEN 10
                 MOVE "Y" TO CANCEL-ENTRY-SW
             WHEN OTHER
                 MOVE "You pressed an invalid Function key."
                     TO MESSAGE-LINE-23.
*
 310-ACCEPT-ACTION-SCREEN.
*
     DISPLAY ACTION-SCREEN.
     ACCEPT ACTION-SCREEN.
```

```
*
 320-EDIT-ACTION-ENTRY.
*
     MOVE SPACE TO ATTRIBUTE-CONTROL-FIELDS.
     MOVE SPACE TO MESSAGE-LINE-23.
     EVALUATE ACTION-CODE
         WHEN 1 THRU 3
             CONTINUE
         WHEN OTHER
             MOVE "N" TO VALID-ACTION-SW
             MOVE "An action code is required."
                 TO MESSAGE-LINE-23
             MOVE 7 TO CURSOR-ROW
             MOVE 26  TO CURSOR-COLUMN.
     IF CM-KEY EQUAL SPACE
         MOVE "N" TO VALID-ACTION-SW
         MOVE "A customer number is required."
             TO MESSAGE-LINE-23
         MOVE 5 TO CURSOR-ROW
     ELSE
         MOVE "Y" TO RECORD-FOUND-SW
         PERFORM 330-READ-CUSTOMER-RECORD
         IF NOT RECORD-FOUND
             IF    CUSTOMER-CHANGE
                OR CUSTOMER-DELETION
                 MOVE "N" TO VALID-ACTION-SW
                 MOVE "Customer record not found for a change or d
-                    "eletion."
                     TO MESSAGE-LINE-23
                 MOVE 5 TO CURSOR-ROW
                 MOVE "HIGHLIGHT" TO CUST-NUMBER-CONTROL.
     IF VALID-ACTION
         IF RECORD-FOUND
             IF CUSTOMER-ADDITION
                 MOVE "N"         TO VALID-ACTION-SW
                 MOVE "Customer record already exists for an addit
-                    "ion."
                     TO MESSAGE-LINE-23
                 MOVE 5 TO CURSOR-ROW
                 MOVE "HIGHLIGHT" TO CUST-NUMBER-CONTROL.
*
 330-READ-CUSTOMER-RECORD.
*
     READ CUSTMAST INTO CUSTOMER-MASTER-RECORD
         INVALID KEY
             MOVE "N" TO RECORD-FOUND-SW.
*
 400-PROCESS-CUSTOMER-ADDITION.
*
     MOVE SPACE   TO CUSTOMER-MASTER-RECORD.
     MOVE CM-KEY TO CM-CUSTOMER-NUMBER.
     MOVE "N"     TO VALID-DATA-SW.
     MOVE "Enter the data for a new customer record."
         TO MESSAGE-LINE-3.
     PERFORM 410-GET-CUSTOMER-DATA
         UNTIL VALID-DATA
             OR CANCEL-ENTRY
             OR END-PROGRAM.
     IF VALID-DATA
         PERFORM 440-WRITE-CUSTOMER-RECORD.
*
```

```
410-GET-CUSTOMER-DATA.
*
    MOVE "Y" TO VALID-DATA-SW.
    PERFORM 420-ACCEPT-CUSTOMER-SCREEN.
    IF ENTER-KEY
        PERFORM 430-EDIT-CUSTOMER-DATA.
    IF FUNCTION-KEY
        MOVE "N" TO VALID-DATA-SW
        EVALUATE FUNCTION-KEY-CODE
            WHEN 3
                MOVE "Y" TO END-PROGRAM-SW
            WHEN 10
                MOVE "Y" TO CANCEL-ENTRY-SW
            WHEN OTHER
                MOVE "You pressed an invalid Function key."
                    TO MESSAGE-LINE-23.
*
420-ACCEPT-CUSTOMER-SCREEN.
*
    DISPLAY CUSTOMER-DATA-SCREEN.
    ACCEPT CUSTOMER-DATA-SCREEN.
*
430-EDIT-CUSTOMER-DATA.
*
    MOVE SPACE TO ATTRIBUTE-CONTROL-FIELDS.
    MOVE SPACE TO MESSAGE-LINE-23.
    IF CM-ZIP-CODE = SPACE
        MOVE "Zip code entry is required." TO MESSAGE-LINE-23
        MOVE 12 TO CURSOR-ROW
        MOVE 26 TO CURSOR-COLUMN.
    IF CM-STATE = SPACE
        MOVE "State code entry is required." TO MESSAGE-LINE-23
        MOVE 11 TO CURSOR-ROW
        MOVE 26 TO CURSOR-COLUMN
    ELSE
        CALL "STATEDIT" USING CM-STATE
                              VALID-STATE-SW
        IF NOT VALID-STATE
            MOVE "Invalid state code" TO MESSAGE-LINE-23
            MOVE "HIGHLIGHT" TO STATE-CONTROL
            MOVE 11 TO CURSOR-ROW
            MOVE 26 TO CURSOR-COLUMN.
    IF MESSAGE-LINE-23 = SPACE
        CALL "ZIPEDIT" USING CM-STATE
                             CM-ZIP-CODE
                             VALID-ZIP-CODE-SW
        IF NOT VALID-ZIP-CODE
            MOVE "Zip code doesn't agree with state code."
                TO MESSAGE-LINE-23
            MOVE "HIGHLIGHT" TO ZIP-CODE-CONTROL
                                STATE-CONTROL
            MOVE 11 TO CURSOR-ROW
            MOVE 26 TO CURSOR-COLUMN.
    IF CM-CITY = SPACE
        MOVE "City entry is required." TO MESSAGE-LINE-23
        MOVE 10 TO CURSOR-ROW
        MOVE 26 TO CURSOR-COLUMN.
    IF CM-ADDRESS = SPACE
        MOVE "Address entry is required." TO MESSAGE-LINE-23
        MOVE  9 TO CURSOR-ROW
        MOVE 26 TO CURSOR-COLUMN.
```

```
            IF  CM-FIRST-NAME = SPACE
                MOVE "First name entry is required." TO MESSAGE-LINE-23
                MOVE  8 TO CURSOR-ROW
                MOVE 26 TO CURSOR-COLUMN.
            IF  CM-LAST-NAME = SPACE
                MOVE "Last name entry is required." TO MESSAGE-LINE-23
                MOVE  7 TO CURSOR-ROW
                MOVE 26 TO CURSOR-COLUMN.
            IF  MESSAGE-LINE-23 NOT = SPACE
                MOVE "N" TO VALID-DATA-SW.
        *
         440-WRITE-CUSTOMER-RECORD.
        *
            WRITE CM-RECORD FROM CUSTOMER-MASTER-RECORD
                INVALID KEY
                    DISPLAY "Invalid WRITE on customer master "
                        CM-KEY.
        *
         500-PROCESS-CUSTOMER-CHANGE.
        *
            MOVE "N" TO VALID-DATA-SW.
            MOVE "Enter the changes to the customer data."
                TO MESSAGE-LINE-3.
            PERFORM 410-GET-CUSTOMER-DATA
                UNTIL VALID-DATA
                    OR CANCEL-ENTRY
                    OR END-PROGRAM.
            IF  VALID-DATA
                PERFORM 510-REWRITE-CUSTOMER-RECORD.
        *
         510-REWRITE-CUSTOMER-RECORD.
        *
            REWRITE CM-RECORD FROM CUSTOMER-MASTER-RECORD
                INVALID KEY
                    DISPLAY "Invalid REWRITE on customer master "
                        CM-KEY.
        *
         600-PROCESS-CUSTOMER-DELETION.
        *
            MOVE "N" TO VALID-DATA-SW.
            MOVE "Press Enter to delete this record."
                TO MESSAGE-LINE-3.
            PERFORM 610-VERIFY-CUSTOMER-DELETION
                UNTIL VALID-DATA
                    OR CANCEL-ENTRY
                    OR END-PROGRAM.
            IF  VALID-DATA
                PERFORM 620-DELETE-CUSTOMER-RECORD.
```

```
*
 610-VERIFY-CUSTOMER-DELETION.
*
     PERFORM 420-ACCEPT-CUSTOMER-SCREEN.
     IF ENTER-KEY
         MOVE "Y" TO VALID-DATA-SW.
     IF FUNCTION-KEY
         EVALUATE FUNCTION-KEY-CODE
             WHEN 3
                 MOVE "Y" TO END-PROGRAM-SW
             WHEN 10
                 MOVE "Y" TO CANCEL-ENTRY-SW
             WHEN OTHER
                 MOVE "You pressed an invalid Function key."
                     TO MESSAGE-LINE-23.
*
 620-DELETE-CUSTOMER-RECORD.
*
     DELETE CUSTMAST
         INVALID KEY
             DISPLAY "Invalid DELETE on customer master "
                 CM-KEY.
```

Program 4

An interactive program that uses CICS on a mainframe

This model program is used to add, delete, or change records in a customer master file. It gets the data that it needs for this maintenance directly from the computer user who is working at a mainframe terminal or workstation. Before the data is used to maintain a record, though, it is edited for completeness and validity.

This program illustrates the use of CICS on a mainframe. If you compare this program with model program 3, which does exactly the same functions, you can see the many differences between a CICS program and an interactive program on another type of computer system. Most of these differences are due to the increased need for processing efficiency on a mainframe, which dictates the need for pseudo-conversational processing.

This model program is taken from *CICS for the COBOL Programmer, Part 1* by Doug Lowe, and it is explained in chapter 5. If you have any trouble understanding how it works, please refer to our CICS book.

Program specifications

Program name	CUSTMNT1	Page	1
Program description	Maintain customer file	Date	11/20/96

Input/output specifications

File name	Description	Format	Use
CUSTMAS	Customer master file	Indexed	I-O
MNTMAP1	Customer key map	Screen	I-O
MNTMAP2	Customer data map	Screen	I-O

Processing specifications

- Control is transferred to this program via an XCTL command from a menu program named INVMENU with no communication area. The user can also start the program by entering the trans-id MNT1. In either case, the program should respond by displaying the customer key map.

- When the key map is displayed, the user enters both a customer key and an action code. If the user selects Add, the customer key must *not* be in the master file. If the user selects Change or Delete, the customer key must be in the master file.

- If the user enters a valid combination of customer key and action, the program displays the data map. For an Add, the user enters the new customer information on this map. For a Change, the user can modify any of the fields that are displayed. For a Deletion, all fields should be set to protected so the user can't enter changes.

- If the user presses PF3 at either the key map or the data map, the program should end and return to the INVMENU by issuing an XCTL command.

- If the user presses PF12 from the key map, the program should also end and return to the menu program. However, if the user presses PF12 from the data map, the program should return to the key map without processing any of the data that was entered.

- For an addition or change, maintain an image of the customer record in the communication area between program executions. If the record is changed in any way between executions, notify the user and do not complete the change or delete operation.

COPY members

CUSTMAS

```
01   CUSTOMER-MASTER-RECORD.
*
     05   CM-CUSTOMER-NUMBER        PIC X(6).
     05   CM-LAST-NAME              PIC X(30).
     05   CM-FIRST-NAME            PIC X(20).
     05   CM-ADDRESS               PIC X(30).
     05   CM-CITY                  PIC X(20).
     05   CM-STATE                 PIC X(2).
     05   CM-ZIP-CODE              PIC X(10).
```

ATTR (improved attribute definitions)

```
01   ATTRIBUTE-DEFINITIONS.
*
     05   ATTR-UNPROT                   PIC X   VALUE X'40'.
     05   ATTR-UNPROT-MDT               PIC X   VALUE X'C1'.
     05   ATTR-UNPROT-BRT               PIC X   VALUE X'C8'.
     05   ATTR-UNPROT-BRT-MDT           PIC X   VALUE X'C9'.
     05   ATTR-UNPROT-DARK              PIC X   VALUE X'4C'.
     05   ATTR-UNPROT-DARK-MDT          PIC X   VALUE X'4D'.
     05   ATTR-UNPROT-NUM               PIC X   VALUE X'50'.
     05   ATTR-UNPROT-NUM-MDT           PIC X   VALUE X'D1'.
     05   ATTR-UNPROT-NUM-BRT           PIC X   VALUE X'D8'.
     05   ATTR-UNPROT-NUM-BRT-MDT       PIC X   VALUE X'D9'.
     05   ATTR-UNPROT-NUM-DARK          PIC X   VALUE X'5C'.
     05   ATTR-UNPROT-NUM-DARK-MDT      PIC X   VALUE X'5D'.
     05   ATTR-PROT                     PIC X   VALUE X'60'.
     05   ATTR-PROT-MDT                 PIC X   VALUE X'61'.
     05   ATTR-PROT-BRT                 PIC X   VALUE X'E8'.
     05   ATTR-PROT-BRT-MDT             PIC X   VALUE X'E9'.
     05   ATTR-PROT-DARK                PIC X   VALUE X'6C'.
     05   ATTR-PROT-DARK-MDT            PIC X   VALUE X'6D'.
     05   ATTR-PROT-SKIP                PIC X   VALUE X'F0'.
     05   ATTR-PROT-SKIP-MDT            PIC X   VALUE X'F1'.
     05   ATTR-PROT-SKIP-BRT            PIC X   VALUE X'F8'.
     05   ATTR-PROT-SKIP-BRT-MDT        PIC X   VALUE X'F9'.
     05   ATTR-PROT-SKIP-DARK           PIC X   VALUE X'7C'.
     05   ATTR-PROT-SKIP-DARK-MDT       PIC X   VALUE X'7D'.
*
     05   ATTR-NO-HIGHLIGHT             PIC X   VALUE X'FF'.
     05   ATTR-BLINK                    PIC X   VALUE '1'.
     05   ATTR-REVERSE                  PIC X   VALUE '2'.
     05   ATTR-UNDERSCORE               PIC X   VALUE '4'.
*
     05   ATTR-DEFAULT-COLOR            PIC X   VALUE X'FF'.
     05   ATTR-BLUE                     PIC X   VALUE '1'.
     05   ATTR-RED                      PIC X   VALUE '2'.
     05   ATTR-PINK                     PIC X   VALUE '3'.
     05   ATTR-GREEN                    PIC X   VALUE '4'.
     05   ATTR-TURQUOISE                PIC X   VALUE '5'.
     05   ATTR-YELLOW                   PIC X   VALUE '6'.
     05   ATTR-NEUTRAL                  PIC X   VALUE '7'.
```

COPY members (continued)

DFHAID (the IBM-supplied definitions for AID keys)

```
01      DFHAID.
    02  DFHNULL     PIC  X   VALUE IS '.'.
    02  DFHENTER    PIC  X   VALUE IS QUOTE.
    02  DFHCLEAR    PIC  X   VALUE IS '_'.
    02  DFHCLRP     PIC  X   VALUE IS '|'.
    02  DFHPEN      PIC  X   VALUE IS '='.
    02  DFHOPID     PIC  X   VALUE IS 'W'.
    02  DFHMSRE     PIC  X   VALUE IS 'X'.
    02  DFHSTRF     PIC  X   VALUE IS 'h'.
    02  DFHTRIG     PIC  X   VALUE IS '"'.
    02  DFHPA1      PIC  X   VALUE IS '%'.
    02  DFHPA2      PIC  X   VALUE IS '>'.
    02  DFHPA3      PIC  X   VALUE IS ','.
    02  DFHPF1      PIC  X   VALUE IS '1'.
    02  DFHPF2      PIC  X   VALUE IS '2'.
    02  DFHPF3      PIC  X   VALUE IS '3'.
    02  DFHPF4      PIC  X   VALUE IS '4'.
    02  DFHPF5      PIC  X   VALUE IS '5'.
    02  DFHPF6      PIC  X   VALUE IS '6'.
    02  DFHPF7      PIC  X   VALUE IS '7'.
    02  DFHPF8      PIC  X   VALUE IS '8'.
    02  DFHPF9      PIC  X   VALUE IS '9'.
    02  DFHPF10     PIC  X   VALUE IS ':'.
    02  DFHPF11     PIC  X   VALUE IS '#'.
    02  DFHPF12     PIC  X   VALUE IS '@'.
    02  DFHPF13     PIC  X   VALUE IS 'A'.
    02  DFHPF14     PIC  X   VALUE IS 'B'.
    02  DFHPF15     PIC  X   VALUE IS 'C'.
    02  DFHPF16     PIC  X   VALUE IS 'D'.
    02  DFHPF17     PIC  X   VALUE IS 'E'.
    02  DFHPF18     PIC  X   VALUE IS 'F'.
    02  DFHPF19     PIC  X   VALUE IS 'G'.
    02  DFHPF20     PIC  X   VALUE IS 'H'.
    02  DFHPF21     PIC  X   VALUE IS 'I'.
    02  DFHPF22     PIC  X   VALUE IS '\'.
    02  DFHPF23     PIC  X   VALUE IS '.'.
    02  DFHPF24     PIC  X   VALUE IS '<'.
```

ERRPARM (parameter definitions for unrecoverable errors)

```
01      ERROR-PARAMETERS.
*
    05  ERR-RESP        PIC  S9(8)      COMP.
    05  ERR-RESP2       PIC  S9(8)      COMP.
    05  ERR-TRNID       PIC  X(4).
    05  ERR-RSRCE       PIC  X(8).
```

Subprograms

- In practice, subprograms would probably be used to edit the state and the zip code entries. For simplicity, though, none are used by this model program.

Screen layouts

Key map

```
              1         2         3         4         5         6         7         8
     12345678901234567890123456789012345678901234567890123456789012345678901234567890
 1 | MNTMAP1          Customer Maintenance
 2 |
 3 | Type a customer number.  Then select an action and press Enter.
 4 |
 5 | Customer number. . . . . XXXXXX
 6 |
 7 | Action . . . . . . . . . X 1.  Add a new customer
 8 |                           2.  Change an existing customer
 9 |                           3.  Delete an existing customer
10 |
11 |
12 |
13 |
14 |
15 |
16 |
17 |
18 |
19 |
20 |
21 |
22 |
23 | XXXXXXXXXXXXXXXXXXXXXXXXXXXXXXXXXXXXXXXXXXXXXXXXXXXXXXXXXXXXXXXXXXXXXXXXXXXX
24 | F3=Exit   F12=Cancel
```

Data map

```
              1         2         3         4         5         6         7         8
     12345678901234567890123456789012345678901234567890123456789012345678901234567890
 1 | MNTMAP2          Customer Maintenance
 2 |
 3 | XXXXXXXXXXXXXXXXXXXXXXXXXXXXXXXXXXXXXXXXXXXXXXXXXXXXXXXXXXXXXXXXXXXXXXXXXXXXXXX
 4 |
 5 | Customer number. . . . . XXXXXX
 6 |
 7 | Last name. . . . . . . . XXXXXXXXXXXXXXXXXXXXXXXXXXXXXX
 8 | First name . . . . . . . XXXXXXXXXXXXXXXXXXXX
 9 | Address. . . . . . . . . XXXXXXXXXXXXXXXXXXXXXXXXXXXXXX
10 | City . . . . . . . . . . XXXXXXXXXXXXXXXXXXXX
11 | State. . . . . . . . . . XX
12 | Zip code . . . . . . . . XXXXXXXXXX
13 |
14 |
15 |
16 |
17 |
18 |
19 |
20 |
21 |
22 |
23 | XXXXXXXXXXXXXXXXXXXXXXXXXXXXXXXXXXXXXXXXXXXXXXXXXXXXXXXXXXXXXXXXXXXXXXXXXXXX
24 | F3=Exit   F12=Cancel
```

The event/response chart

Program name	CUSTMNT1		Page	1
Program description	Maintain customer file		Date	11/20/96

Event/response summary

Event	Context	Response	New context
Program start	N/A	Display the key map.	Get key
PF3	All	Return to the menu program.	N/A
PF12	Get key	Return to the menu program.	N/A
	Add customer Change customer Delete customer	Cancel operation and display the key map.	Get key
Enter	Get key	Edit input data. If valid display the data map	Add customer, Change customer, or Delete customer
		Else display an error message.	Get key
	Add customer	Edit input data. If valid add the customer record display the key map	Get key
		Else display an error message.	Add customer
	Change customer	Edit input data. If valid change customer record display the key map	Get key
		Else display an error message.	Change customer
	Delete customer	Delete the customer record. Display the key map.	Get key
Clear	All	Redisplay the current map.	Unchanged
PA1, PA2, or PA3	All	Ignore the key.	Unchanged
Other key	All	Display an error message.	Unchanged

The structure chart

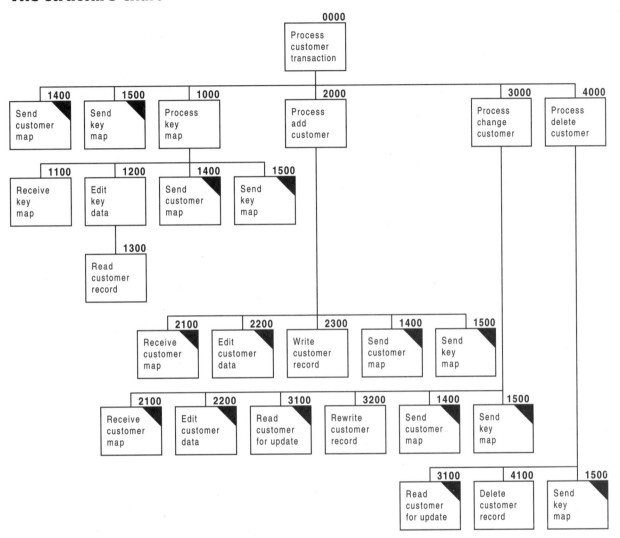

Mapset listing

```
            PRINT NOGEN
    MNTSET1 DFHMSD TYPE=&SYSPARM,                                          X
                LANG=COBOL,                                               X
                MODE=INOUT,                                               X
                TERM=3270-2,                                              X
                CTRL=FREEKB,                                              X
                STORAGE=AUTO,                                             X
                DSATTS=(COLOR,HILIGHT),                                   X
                MAPATTS=(COLOR,HILIGHT),                                  X
                TIOAPFX=YES
    ********************************************************************
    MNTMAP1 DFHMDI SIZE=(24,80),                                          X
                LINE=1,                                                   X
                COLUMN=1
    ********************************************************************
            DFHMDF POS=(1,1),                                             X
                LENGTH=7,                                                 X
                ATTRB=(NORM,PROT),                                        X
                COLOR=BLUE,                                               X
                INITIAL='MNTMAP1'
            DFHMDF POS=(1,20),                                            X
                LENGTH=20,                                                X
                ATTRB=(NORM,PROT),                                        X
                COLOR=BLUE,                                               X
                INITIAL='Customer Maintenance'
    ********************************************************************
            DFHMDF POS=(3,1),                                             X
                LENGTH=63,                                                X
                ATTRB=(NORM,PROT),                                        X
                COLOR=GREEN,                                              X
                INITIAL='Type a customer number.  Then select an action X
                and press Enter.'
            DFHMDF POS=(5,1),                                             X
                LENGTH=24,                                                X
                ATTRB=(NORM,PROT),                                        X
                COLOR=GREEN,                                              X
                INITIAL='Customer number. . . . .'
    CUSTNO1 DFHMDF POS=(5,26),                                            X
                LENGTH=6,                                                 X
                ATTRB=(NORM,UNPROT,FSET,IC),                              X
                COLOR=TURQUOISE,                                          X
                INITIAL='_____'
            DFHMDF POS=(5,33),                                            X
                LENGTH=1,                                                 X
                ATTRB=ASKIP
            DFHMDF POS=(7,1),                                             X
                LENGTH=24,                                                X
                ATTRB=(NORM,PROT),                                        X
                COLOR=GREEN,                                              X
                INITIAL='Action . . . . . . . . .'
    ACTION  DFHMDF POS=(7,26),                                            X
                LENGTH=1,                                                 X
                ATTRB=(NORM,UNPROT,FSET),                                 X
                COLOR=TURQUOISE,                                          X
                  INITIAL='_'
            DFHMDF POS=(7,28),                                            X
                LENGTH=21,                                                X
                ATTRB=(NORM,ASKIP),                                       X
                COLOR=NEUTRAL,                                            X
```

```
                            INITIAL='1. Add a new customer'
              DFHMDF POS=(8,28),                                           X
                     LENGTH=30,                                           X
                     ATTRB=(NORM,ASKIP),                                  X
                     COLOR=NEUTRAL,                                       X
                     INITIAL='2. Change an existing customer'
              DFHMDF POS=(9,28),                                           X
                     LENGTH=21,                                           X
                     ATTRB=(NORM,ASKIP),                                  X
                     COLOR=NEUTRAL,                                       X
                     INITIAL='3. Delete an existing customer'
MSG1          DFHMDF POS=(23,1),                                          X
                     LENGTH=79,                                           X
                     ATTRB=(BRT,PROT),                                    X
                     COLOR=YELLOW
              DFHMDF POS=(24,1),                                          X
                     LENGTH=20,                                           X
                     ATTRB=(NORM,PROT),                                   X
                     COLOR=BLUE,                                          X
                     INITIAL='F3=Exit    F12=Cancel'
DUMMY1        DFHMDF POS=(24,79),                                         X
                     LENGTH=1,                                            X
                     ATTRB=(DRK,PROT,FSET),                               X
                     INITIAL=' '
********************************************************************
MNTMAP2   DFHMDI SIZE=(24,80),                                            X
                     LINE=1,                                              X
                     COLUMN=1
********************************************************************
              DFHMDF POS=(1,1),                                           X
                     LENGTH=7,                                            X
                     ATTRB=(NORM,PROT),                                   X
                     COLOR=BLUE,                                          X
                     INITIAL='MNTMAP2'
              DFHMDF POS=(1,20),                                          X
                     LENGTH=20,                                           X
                     ATTRB=(NORM,PROT),                                   X
                     COLOR=BLUE,                                          X
                     INITIAL='Customer Maintenance'
********************************************************************
INSTR2        DFHMDF POS=(3,1),                                           X
                     LENGTH=79,                                           X
                     ATTRB=(NORM,PROT),                                   X
                     COLOR=GREEN
              DFHMDF POS=(5,1),                                           X
                     LENGTH=24,                                           X
                     ATTRB=(NORM,PROT),                                   X
                     COLOR=GREEN,                                         X
                     INITIAL='Customer number. . . . :'
CUSTNO2       DFHMDF POS=(5,26),                                          X
                     LENGTH=6,                                            X
                     ATTRB=(NORM,PROT,FSET,IC),                           X
                     COLOR=TURQUOISE
********************************************************************
              DFHMDF POS=(7,1),                                           X
                     LENGTH=24,                                           X
                     ATTRB=(NORM,PROT),                                   X
                     COLOR=GREEN,                                         X
                     INITIAL='Last name. . . . . . . :'
LNAME         DFHMDF POS=(7,26),                                          X
                     LENGTH=30,                                           X
```

```
                         ATTRB=(NORM,UNPROT,FSET),                            X
                         COLOR=TURQUOISE
               DFHMDF POS=(7,57),                                            X
                         LENGTH=1,                                           X
                         ATTRB=ASKIP
****************************************************************************
               DFHMDF POS=(8,1),                                            X
                         LENGTH=24,                                         X
                         ATTRB=(NORM,PROT),                                 X
                         COLOR=GREEN,                                       X
                         INITIAL='First name . . . . . . .'
FNAME          DFHMDF POS=(8,26),                                           X
                         LENGTH=20,                                         X
                         ATTRB=(NORM,UNPROT,FSET),                          X
                         COLOR=TURQUOISE
               DFHMDF POS=(8,47),                                           X
                         LENGTH=1,                                          X
                         ATTRB=ASKIP
****************************************************************************
               DFHMDF POS=(9,1),                                            X
                         LENGTH=24,                                         X
                         ATTRB=(NORM,PROT),                                 X
                         COLOR=GREEN,                                       X
                         INITIAL='Address. . . . . . . . .'
ADDR           DFHMDF POS=(9,26),                                           X
                         LENGTH=30,                                         X
                         ATTRB=(NORM,UNPROT,FSET),                          X
                         COLOR=TURQUOISE
               DFHMDF POS=(9,57),                                           X
                         LENGTH=1,                                          X
                         ATTRB=ASKIP
****************************************************************************
               DFHMDF POS=(10,1),                                           X
                         LENGTH=24,                                         X
                         ATTRB=(NORM,PROT),                                 X
                         COLOR=GREEN,                                       X
                         INITIAL='City . . . . . . . . . .'
CITY           DFHMDF POS=(10,26),                                          X
                         LENGTH=20,                                         X
                         ATTRB=(NORM,UNPROT,FSET),                          X
                         COLOR=TURQUOISE
               DFHMDF POS=(10,47),                                          X
                         LENGTH=1,                                          X
                         ATTRB=ASKIP
****************************************************************************
               DFHMDF POS=(11,1),                                           X
                         LENGTH=24,                                         X
                         ATTRB=(NORM,PROT),                                 X
                         COLOR=GREEN,                                       X
                         INITIAL='State. . . . . . . . . .'
STATE          DFHMDF POS=(11,26),                                          X
                         LENGTH=2,                                          X
                         ATTRB=(NORM,UNPROT,FSET),                          X
                         COLOR=TURQUOISE
               DFHMDF POS=(11,29),                                          X
                         LENGTH=1,                                          X
                         ATTRB=ASKIP
****************************************************************************
               DFHMDF POS=(12,1),                                           X
                         LENGTH=24,                                         X
                         ATTRB=(NORM,PROT),                                 X
```

```
                        COLOR=GREEN,                                             X
                        INITIAL='Zip Code . . . . . . . .'
ZIPCODE    DFHMDF POS=(12,26),                                                   X
                        LENGTH=10,                                               X
                        ATTRB=(NORM,UNPROT,FSET),                                X
                        COLOR=TURQUOISE
           DFHMDF POS=(12,37),                                                   X
                        LENGTH=1,                                                X
                        ATTRB=ASKIP
***********************************************************************
MSG2       DFHMDF POS=(23,1),                                                    X
                        LENGTH=79,                                               X
                        ATTRB=(BRT,PROT),                                        X
                        COLOR=YELLOW
           DFHMDF POS=(24,1),                                                    X
                        LENGTH=20,                                               X
                        ATTRB=(NORM,PROT),                                       X
                        COLOR=BLUE,                                              X
                        INITIAL='F3=Exit     F12=Cancel'
DUMMY2     DFHMDF POS=(24,79),                                                   X
                        LENGTH=1,                                                X
                        ATTRB=(DRK,PROT,FSET),                                   X
                        INITIAL=' '
***********************************************************************
           DFHMSD TYPE=FINAL
           END
```

BMS-generated symbolic maps

```
01   MNTMAP1I.
     02    FILLER    PIC X(12).
     02    CUSTNO1L  PIC S9(4) COMP.
     02    CUSTNO1F  PIC X.
     02    FILLER REDEFINES CUSTNO1F.
      03   CUSTNO1A  PIC X.
     02    FILLER    PIC X(0002).
     02    CUSTNO1I  PIC X(0006).
     02    ACTIONL   PIC S9(4) COMP.
     02    ACTIONF   PIC X.
     02    FILLER REDEFINES ACTIONF.
      03   ACTIONA   PIC X.
     02    FILLER    PIC X(0002).
     02    ACTIONI   PIC X(0001).
     02    MSG1L     PIC S9(4) COMP.
     02    MSG1F     PIC X.
     02    FILLER REDEFINES MSG1F.
      03   MSG1A     PIC X.
     02    FILLER    PIC X(0002).
     02    MSG1I     PIC X(0079).
     02    DUMMY1L   PIC S9(4) COMP.
     02    DUMMY1F   PIC X.
     02    FILLER REDEFINES DUMMY1F.
      03   DUMMY1A   PIC X.
     02    FILLER    PIC X(0002).
     02    DUMMY1I   PIC X(0001).
01   MNTMAP1O REDEFINES MNTMAP1I.
     02    FILLER    PIC X(12).
     02    FILLER    PIC X(3).
     02    CUSTNO1C  PIC X.
     02    CUSTNO1H  PIC X.
     02    CUSTNO1O  PIC X(0006).
     02    FILLER    PIC X(3).
     02    ACTIONC   PIC X.
     02    ACTIONH   PIC X.
     02    ACTIONO   PIC X(0001).
     02    FILLER    PIC X(3).
     02    MSG1C     PIC X.
     02    MSG1H     PIC X.
     02    MSG1O     PIC X(0079).
     02    FILLER    PIC X(3).
     02    DUMMY1C   PIC X.
     02    DUMMY1H   PIC X.
     02    DUMMY1O   PIC X(0001).
01   MNTMAP2I.
     02    FILLER    PIC X(12).
     02    INSTR2L   PIC S9(4) COMP.
     02    INSTR2F   PIC X.
     02    FILLER REDEFINES INSTR2F.
      03   INSTR2A   PIC X.
     02    FILLER    PIC X(0002).
     02    INSTR2I   PIC X(0079).
     02    CUSTNO2L  PIC S9(4) COMP.
     02    CUSTNO2F  PIC X.
     02    FILLER REDEFINES CUSTNO2F.
      03   CUSTNO2A  PIC X.
     02    FILLER    PIC X(0002).
     02    CUSTNO2I  PIC X(0006).
     02    LNAMEL    PIC S9(4) COMP.
```

```
02   LNAMEF    PIC X.
02   FILLER REDEFINES LNAMEF.
 03  LNAMEA    PIC X.
02   FILLER    PIC X(0002).
02   LNAMEI    PIC X(0030).
02   FNAMEL    PIC S9(4) COMP.
02   FNAMEF    PIC X.
02   FILLER REDEFINES FNAMEF.
 03  FNAMEA    PIC X.
02   FILLER    PIC X(0002).
02   FNAMEI    PIC X(0020).
02   ADDRL     PIC S9(4) COMP.
02   ADDRF     PIC X.
02   FILLER REDEFINES ADDRF.
 03  ADDRA     PIC X.
02   FILLER    PIC X(0002).
02   ADDRI     PIC X(0030).
02   CITYL     PIC S9(4) COMP.
02   CITYF     PIC X.
02   FILLER REDEFINES CITYF.
 03  CITYA     PIC X.
02   FILLER    PIC X(0002).
02   CITYI     PIC X(0020).
02   STATEL    PIC S9(4) COMP.
02   STATEF    PIC X.
02   FILLER REDEFINES STATEF.
 03  STATEA    PIC X.
02   FILLER    PIC X(0002).
02   STATEI    PIC X(0002).
02   ZIPCODEL  PIC S9(4) COMP.
02   ZIPCODEF  PIC X.
02   FILLER REDEFINES ZIPCODEF.
 03  ZIPCODEA  PIC X.
02   FILLER    PIC X(0002).
02   ZIPCODEI  PIC X(0010).
02   MSG2L     PIC S9(4) COMP.
02   MSG2F     PIC X.
02   FILLER REDEFINES MSG2F.
 03  MSG2A     PIC X.
02   FILLER    PIC X(0002).
02   MSG2I     PIC X(0079).
02   DUMMY2L   PIC S9(4) COMP.
02   DUMMY2F   PIC X.
02   FILLER REDEFINES DUMMY2F.
 03  DUMMY2A   PIC X.
 02  FILLER    PIC X(0002).
02   DUMMY2I   PIC X(0001).
01 MNTMAP20 REDEFINES MNTMAP2I.
02   FILLER    PIC X(12).
02   FILLER    PIC X(3).
02   INSTR2C   PIC X.
02   INSTR2H   PIC X.
02   INSTR20   PIC X(0079).
02   FILLER    PIC X(3).
02   CUSTNO2C  PIC X.
02   CUSTNO2H  PIC X.
02   CUSTNO20  PIC X(0006).
02   FILLER    PIC X(3).
02   LNAMEC    PIC X.
02   LNAMEH    PIC X.
02   LNAMEO    PIC X(0030).
```

```
02    FILLER      PIC X(3).
02    FNAMEC      PIC X.
02    FNAMEH      PIC X.
02    FNAMEO      PIC X(0020).
02    FILLER      PIC X(3).
02    ADDRC       PIC X.
02    ADDRH       PIC X.
02    ADDRO       PIC X(0030).
02    FILLER      PIC X(3).
02    CITYC       PIC X.
02    CITYH       PIC X.
02    CITYO       PIC X(0020).
02    FILLER      PIC X(3).
02    STATEC      PIC X.
02    STATEH      PIC X.
02    STATEO      PIC X(0002).
02    FILLER      PIC X(3).
02    ZIPCODEC    PIC X.
02    ZIPCODEH    PIC X.
02    ZIPCODEO    PIC X(0010).
02    FILLER      PIC X(3).
02    MSG2C       PIC X.
02    MSG2H       PIC X.
02    MSG2O       PIC X(0079).
02    FILLER      PIC X(3).
02    DUMMY2C     PIC X.
02    DUMMY2H     PIC X.
02    DUMMY2O     PIC X(0001).
```

Source listing

```
      IDENTIFICATION DIVISION.
*
      PROGRAM-ID.     CUSTMNT1.
*
      ENVIRONMENT DIVISION.
*
      DATA DIVISION.
*
      WORKING-STORAGE SECTION.
*
      01   SWITCHES.
*
          05   VALID-DATA-SW              PIC X    VALUE 'Y'.
               88   VALID-DATA                     VALUE 'Y'.
*
      01   FLAGS.
*
          05   SEND-FLAG                  PIC X.
               88   SEND-ERASE                     VALUE '1'.
               88   SEND-ERASE-ALARM               VALUE '2'.
               88   SEND-DATAONLY                  VALUE '3'.
               88   SEND-DATAONLY-ALARM            VALUE '4'.
*
      01   WORK-FIELDS.
*
          05   RESPONSE-CODE              PIC S9(8) COMP.
*
      01   COMMUNICATION-AREA.
*
          05   CA-CONTEXT-FLAG            PIC X.
               88   PROCESS-KEY-MAP                VALUE '1'.
               88   PROCESS-ADD-CUSTOMER           VALUE '2'.
               88   PROCESS-CHANGE-CUSTOMER        VALUE '3'.
               88   PROCESS-DELETE-CUSTOMER        VALUE '4'.
          05   CA-CUSTOMER-RECORD.
               10   CA-CUSTOMER-NUMBER     PIC X(6).
               10   FILLER                 PIC X(112).
*
      COPY CUSTMAS.
*
      COPY MNTSET1.
*
      COPY ATTR.
*
      COPY DFHAID.
*
      COPY ERRPARM.
*
      LINKAGE SECTION.
*
      01   DFHCOMMAREA                    PIC X(119).
*
      PROCEDURE DIVISION.
*
      0000-PROCESS-CUSTOMER-TRANSACTION.
*
          MOVE DFHCOMMAREA TO COMMUNICATION-AREA.
          EVALUATE TRUE
              WHEN EIBCALEN = ZERO
```

```
                        MOVE LOW-VALUE TO MNTMAP1O
                        MOVE -1 TO CUSTNO1L
                        SET SEND-ERASE TO TRUE
                        PERFORM 1500-SEND-KEY-MAP
                        SET PROCESS-KEY-MAP TO TRUE
                    WHEN EIBAID = DFHPF3
                        EXEC CICS
                            XCTL PROGRAM('INVMENU')
                        END-EXEC
                    WHEN EIBAID = DFHPF12
                        IF PROCESS-KEY-MAP
                            EXEC CICS
                                XCTL PROGRAM('INVMENU')
                            END-EXEC
                        ELSE
                            MOVE LOW-VALUE TO MNTMAP1O
                            MOVE -1 TO CUSTNO1L
                            SET SEND-ERASE TO TRUE
                            PERFORM 1500-SEND-KEY-MAP
                            SET PROCESS-KEY-MAP TO TRUE
                    WHEN EIBAID = DFHCLEAR
                        IF PROCESS-KEY-MAP
                            MOVE LOW-VALUE TO MNTMAP1O
                            MOVE -1 TO CUSTNO1L
                            SET SEND-ERASE TO TRUE
                            PERFORM 1500-SEND-KEY-MAP
                        ELSE
                            MOVE LOW-VALUE TO MNTMAP2O
                            MOVE -1 TO CUSTNO2L
                            SET SEND-ERASE TO TRUE
                            PERFORM 1400-SEND-CUSTOMER-MAP
                    WHEN EIBAID = DFHPA1 OR DFHPA2 OR DFHPA3
                        CONTINUE
                    WHEN EIBAID = DFHENTER
                        IF PROCESS-KEY-MAP
                            PERFORM 1000-PROCESS-KEY-MAP
                        ELSE IF PROCESS-ADD-CUSTOMER
                            PERFORM 2000-PROCESS-ADD-CUSTOMER
                        ELSE IF PROCESS-CHANGE-CUSTOMER
                            PERFORM 3000-PROCESS-CHANGE-CUSTOMER
                        ELSE IF PROCESS-DELETE-CUSTOMER
                            PERFORM 4000-PROCESS-DELETE-CUSTOMER
                    WHEN OTHER
                        IF PROCESS-KEY-MAP
                            MOVE LOW-VALUE TO MNTMAP1O
                            MOVE -1 TO CUSTNO1L
                            MOVE 'That key is unassigned.' TO MSG10
                            SET SEND-DATAONLY-ALARM TO TRUE
                            PERFORM 1500-SEND-KEY-MAP
                        ELSE
                            MOVE LOW-VALUE TO MNTMAP2O
                            MOVE -1 TO CUSTNO2L
                            MOVE 'That key is unassigned.' TO MSG20
                            SET SEND-DATAONLY-ALARM TO TRUE
                            PERFORM 1400-SEND-CUSTOMER-MAP
                END-EVALUATE.
                EXEC CICS
                    RETURN TRANSID('MNT1')
                            COMMAREA(COMMUNICATION-AREA)
                END-EXEC.
            *
```

```
     1000-PROCESS-KEY-MAP.
*
     PERFORM 1100-RECEIVE-KEY-MAP.
     PERFORM 1200-EDIT-KEY-DATA.
     IF VALID-DATA
         INSPECT CUSTOMER-MASTER-RECORD
             REPLACING ALL SPACE BY '_'
         MOVE CUSTNO1I       TO CUSTNO2O
         MOVE CM-LAST-NAME   TO LNAMEO
         MOVE CM-FIRST-NAME  TO FNAMEO
         MOVE CM-ADDRESS     TO ADDRO
         MOVE CM-CITY        TO CITYO
         MOVE CM-STATE       TO STATEO
         MOVE CM-ZIP-CODE    TO ZIPCODEO
         MOVE -1             TO LNAMEL
         SET SEND-ERASE TO TRUE
         PERFORM 1400-SEND-CUSTOMER-MAP
     ELSE
         MOVE LOW-VALUE TO CUSTNO1O
                           ACTIONO
         SET SEND-DATAONLY-ALARM TO TRUE
         PERFORM 1500-SEND-KEY-MAP.
*
 1100-RECEIVE-KEY-MAP.
*
     EXEC CICS
         RECEIVE MAP('MNTMAP1')
                 MAPSET('MNTSET1')
                 INTO(MNTMAP1I)
     END-EXEC.
     INSPECT MNTMAP1I
         REPLACING ALL '_' BY SPACE.
*
 1200-EDIT-KEY-DATA.
*
     MOVE ATTR-NO-HIGHLIGHT TO ACTIONH
                               CUSTNO1H.
     IF ACTIONI NOT = '1' AND '2' AND '3'
         MOVE ATTR-REVERSE TO ACTIONH
         MOVE -1 TO ACTIONL
         MOVE 'Action must be 1, 2, or 3.' TO MSG10
         MOVE 'N' TO VALID-DATA-SW.
     IF        CUSTNO1L = ZERO
         OR CUSTNO1I = SPACE
         MOVE ATTR-REVERSE TO CUSTNO1H
         MOVE -1 TO CUSTNO1L
         MOVE 'You must enter a customer number.' TO MSG10
         MOVE 'N' TO VALID-DATA-SW.
     IF VALID-DATA
         EVALUATE ACTIONI
             WHEN '1'
                 PERFORM 1300-READ-CUSTOMER-RECORD
                 IF RESPONSE-CODE = DFHRESP(NOTFND)
                     MOVE 'Type information for new customer.  The
-                         'n press Enter.' TO INSTR2O
                     SET PROCESS-ADD-CUSTOMER TO TRUE
                     MOVE SPACE TO CUSTOMER-MASTER-RECORD
                 ELSE
                     MOVE 'That customer already exists.'
                         TO MSG10
                     MOVE 'N' TO VALID-DATA-SW
```

```
                        WHEN '2'
                            PERFORM 1300-READ-CUSTOMER-RECORD
                            IF RESPONSE-CODE = DFHRESP(NORMAL)
                                MOVE 'Type changes.  Then press Enter.'
                                    TO INSTR20
                                SET PROCESS-CHANGE-CUSTOMER TO TRUE
                            ELSE
                                MOVE 'That customer does not exist.' TO MSG10
                                MOVE 'N' TO VALID-DATA-SW
                        WHEN '3'
                            PERFORM 1300-READ-CUSTOMER-RECORD
                            IF RESPONSE-CODE = DFHRESP(NORMAL)
                                MOVE 'Press Enter to delete this customer or
                                    'press F12 to cancel.' TO INSTR20
                                SET PROCESS-DELETE-CUSTOMER TO TRUE
                                MOVE ATTR-PROT TO LNAMEA
                                                 FNAMEA
                                                 ADDRA
                                                 CITYA
                                                 STATEA
                                                 ZIPCODEA
                            ELSE
                                MOVE 'That customer does not exist.' TO MSG10
                                MOVE 'N' TO VALID-DATA-SW
                    END-EVALUATE.
    *
      1300-READ-CUSTOMER-RECORD.
    *
          EXEC CICS
              READ DATASET('CUSTMAS')
                   INTO(CUSTOMER-MASTER-RECORD)
                   RIDFLD(CUSTNO1I)
                   RESP(RESPONSE-CODE)
          END-EXEC.
          IF        RESPONSE-CODE NOT = DFHRESP(NORMAL)
              AND   RESPONSE-CODE NOT = DFHRESP(NOTFND)
              GO TO 9999-TERMINATE-PROGRAM.
          MOVE CUSTOMER-MASTER-RECORD TO CA-CUSTOMER-RECORD.
    *
      1400-SEND-CUSTOMER-MAP.
    *
          EVALUATE TRUE
              WHEN SEND-ERASE
                  EXEC CICS
                      SEND MAP('MNTMAP2')
                           MAPSET('MNTSET1')
                           FROM(MNTMAP20)
                           ERASE
                           CURSOR
                  END-EXEC
              WHEN SEND-DATAONLY-ALARM
                  EXEC CICS
                      SEND MAP('MNTMAP2')
                           MAPSET('MNTSET1')
                           FROM(MNTMAP20)
                           DATAONLY
                           ALARM
                           CURSOR
                  END-EXEC
          END-EVALUATE.
    *
```

```
     1500-SEND-KEY-MAP.
*
         EVALUATE TRUE
             WHEN SEND-ERASE
                 EXEC CICS
                     SEND MAP('MNTMAP1')
                          MAPSET('MNTSET1')
                          FROM(MNTMAP10)
                          ERASE
                          CURSOR
                 END-EXEC
             WHEN SEND-ERASE-ALARM
                 EXEC CICS
                     SEND MAP('MNTMAP1')
                          MAPSET('MNTSET1')
                          FROM(MNTMAP10)
                          ERASE
                          ALARM
                          CURSOR
                 END-EXEC
             WHEN SEND-DATAONLY-ALARM
                 EXEC CICS
                     SEND MAP('MNTMAP1')
                          MAPSET('MNTSET1')
                          FROM(MNTMAP10)
                          DATAONLY
                          ALARM
                          CURSOR
             END-EXEC
         END-EVALUATE.
*
     2000-PROCESS-ADD-CUSTOMER.
*
         PERFORM 2100-RECEIVE-CUSTOMER-MAP.
         PERFORM 2200-EDIT-CUSTOMER-DATA.
         IF VALID-DATA
             PERFORM 2300-WRITE-CUSTOMER-RECORD
             IF RESPONSE-CODE = DFHRESP(NORMAL)
                 MOVE 'Customer record added.' TO MSG10
                 SET SEND-ERASE TO TRUE
             ELSE
                 MOVE 'Another user has added a record with that custo
-                     'mer number.' TO MSG10
                 SET SEND-ERASE-ALARM TO TRUE
             END-IF
             PERFORM 1500-SEND-KEY-MAP
             SET PROCESS-KEY-MAP TO TRUE
         ELSE
             MOVE LOW-VALUE TO LNAMEO
                               FNAMEO
                               ADDRO
                               CITYO
                               STATEO
                               ZIPCODEO
             SET SEND-DATAONLY-ALARM TO TRUE
             PERFORM 1400-SEND-CUSTOMER-MAP.
```

```
*
 2100-RECEIVE-CUSTOMER-MAP.
*
     EXEC CICS
         RECEIVE MAP('MNTMAP2')
                 MAPSET('MNTSET1')
                 INTO(MNTMAP2I)
     END-EXEC.
     INSPECT MNTMAP2I
         REPLACING ALL '_' BY SPACE.
*
 2200-EDIT-CUSTOMER-DATA.
*
     MOVE ATTR-NO-HIGHLIGHT TO ZIPCODEH
                               STATEH
                               CITYH
                               ADDRH
                               FNAMEH
                               LNAMEH.
     IF       ZIPCODEI = SPACE
        OR ZIPCODEL = ZERO
        MOVE ATTR-REVERSE TO ZIPCODEH
        MOVE -1 TO ZIPCODEL
        MOVE 'You must enter a zip code.' TO MSG20
        MOVE 'N' TO VALID-DATA-SW.
     IF       STATEI = SPACE
        OR STATEL = ZERO
        MOVE ATTR-REVERSE TO STATEH
        MOVE -1 TO STATEL
        MOVE 'You must enter a state.' TO MSG20
        MOVE 'N' TO VALID-DATA-SW.
     IF       CITYI = SPACE
        OR CITYL = ZERO
        MOVE ATTR-REVERSE TO CITYH
        MOVE -1 TO CITYL
        MOVE 'You must enter a city.' TO MSG20
        MOVE 'N' TO VALID-DATA-SW.
     IF       ADDRI = SPACE
        OR ADDRL = ZERO
        MOVE ATTR-REVERSE TO ADDRH
        MOVE -1 TO ADDRL
        MOVE 'You must enter an address.' TO MSG20
        MOVE 'N' TO VALID-DATA-SW.
     IF       FNAMEI = SPACE
        OR FNAMEL = ZERO
        MOVE ATTR-REVERSE TO FNAMEH
        MOVE -1 TO FNAMEL
        MOVE 'You must enter a first name.' TO MSG20
        MOVE 'N' TO VALID-DATA-SW.
     IF       LNAMEI = SPACE
        OR LNAMEL = ZERO
        MOVE ATTR-REVERSE TO LNAMEH
        MOVE -1 TO LNAMEL
        MOVE 'You must enter a last name.' TO MSG20
        MOVE 'N' TO VALID-DATA-SW.
```

```
*
 2300-WRITE-CUSTOMER-RECORD.
*
     MOVE CUSTNO2I TO CM-CUSTOMER-NUMBER.
     MOVE LNAMEI    TO CM-LAST-NAME.
     MOVE FNAMEI    TO CM-FIRST-NAME.
     MOVE ADDRI     TO CM-ADDRESS.
     MOVE CITYI     TO CM-CITY.
     MOVE STATEI    TO CM-STATE.
     MOVE ZIPCODEI TO CM-ZIP-CODE.
     EXEC CICS
         WRITE DATASET('CUSTMAS')
               FROM(CUSTOMER-MASTER-RECORD)
               RIDFLD(CM-CUSTOMER-NUMBER)
               RESP(RESPONSE-CODE)
     END-EXEC.
     IF        RESPONSE-CODE NOT = DFHRESP(NORMAL)
         AND RESPONSE-CODE NOT = DFHRESP(DUPREC)
         GO TO 9999-TERMINATE-PROGRAM.
*
 3000-PROCESS-CHANGE-CUSTOMER.
*
     PERFORM 2100-RECEIVE-CUSTOMER-MAP.
     PERFORM 2200-EDIT-CUSTOMER-DATA.
     IF VALID-DATA
         MOVE CUSTNO2I TO CM-CUSTOMER-NUMBER
         PERFORM 3100-READ-CUSTOMER-FOR-UPDATE
         IF RESPONSE-CODE = DFHRESP(NORMAL)
             IF CUSTOMER-MASTER-RECORD = CA-CUSTOMER-RECORD
                 PERFORM 3200-REWRITE-CUSTOMER-RECORD
                 MOVE 'Customer record updated.' TO MSG10
                 SET SEND-ERASE TO TRUE
             ELSE
                 MOVE 'Another user has updated the record.  Try a
-                     'gain.' TO MSG10
                 SET SEND-ERASE-ALARM TO TRUE
         ELSE
             MOVE 'Another user has deleted the record.' TO MSG10
             SET SEND-ERASE-ALARM TO TRUE
         END-IF
         PERFORM 1500-SEND-KEY-MAP
         SET PROCESS-KEY-MAP TO TRUE
     ELSE
         SET SEND-DATAONLY-ALARM TO TRUE
         PERFORM 1400-SEND-CUSTOMER-MAP.
*
 3100-READ-CUSTOMER-FOR-UPDATE.
*
     EXEC CICS
         READ DATASET('CUSTMAS')
              INTO(CUSTOMER-MASTER-RECORD)
              RIDFLD(CM-CUSTOMER-NUMBER)
              UPDATE
              RESP(RESPONSE-CODE)
     END-EXEC.
     IF        RESPONSE-CODE NOT = DFHRESP(NORMAL)
         AND RESPONSE-CODE NOT = DFHRESP(NOTFND)
         GO TO 9999-TERMINATE-PROGRAM.
```

```
*
 3200-REWRITE-CUSTOMER-RECORD.
*
     MOVE LNAMEI    TO CM-LAST-NAME.
     MOVE FNAMEI    TO CM-FIRST-NAME.
     MOVE ADDRI     TO CM-ADDRESS.
     MOVE CITYI     TO CM-CITY.
     MOVE STATEI    TO CM-STATE.
     MOVE ZIPCODEI TO CM-ZIP-CODE.
     EXEC CICS
         REWRITE DATASET('CUSTMAS')
                 FROM(CUSTOMER-MASTER-RECORD)
                 RESP(RESPONSE-CODE)
     END-EXEC.
     IF RESPONSE-CODE NOT = DFHRESP(NORMAL)
         GO TO 9999-TERMINATE-PROGRAM.
*
 4000-PROCESS-DELETE-CUSTOMER.
*
     MOVE CA-CUSTOMER-NUMBER TO CM-CUSTOMER-NUMBER.
     PERFORM 3100-READ-CUSTOMER-FOR-UPDATE.
     IF RESPONSE-CODE = DFHRESP(NORMAL)
         IF CUSTOMER-MASTER-RECORD = CA-CUSTOMER-RECORD
             PERFORM 4100-DELETE-CUSTOMER-RECORD
             MOVE 'Customer deleted.' TO MSG10
             SET SEND-ERASE TO TRUE
         ELSE
             MOVE 'Another user has updated the record.  Try again
-                '.' TO MSG10
             SET SEND-ERASE-ALARM TO TRUE
     ELSE
         MOVE 'Another user has deleted the record.' TO MSG10
         SET SEND-ERASE-ALARM TO TRUE.
     PERFORM 1500-SEND-KEY-MAP.
     SET PROCESS-KEY-MAP TO TRUE.
*
 4100-DELETE-CUSTOMER-RECORD.
*
     EXEC CICS
         DELETE DATASET('CUSTMAS')
                RESP(RESPONSE-CODE)
     END-EXEC.
     IF          RESPONSE-CODE NOT = DFHRESP(NORMAL)
         GO TO 9999-TERMINATE-PROGRAM.
*
 9999-TERMINATE-PROGRAM.
*
     MOVE EIBRESP  TO ERR-RESP.
     MOVE EIBRESP2 TO ERR-RESP2.
     MOVE EIBTRNID TO ERR-TRNID.
     MOVE EIBRSRCE TO ERR-RSRCE.
     EXEC CICS
         XCTL PROGRAM('SYSERR')
              COMMAREA(ERROR-PARAMETERS)
     END-EXEC.
```

Program 5

A report preparation
program that uses
DB2 and SQL
on a mainframe

This model program shows how you can use the principles and methods presented in this book to implement DB2 programs on a mainframe. It's a simple program that prints an invoice register from a DB2 database. The data that's needed for this register is taken from two DB2 tables (a customer table and an invoice table) that are joined by customer number.

This program is taken from *DB2 for the COBOL Programmer, Part 1* by Steve Eckols. If you have any trouble understanding how this model program works, please refer to that book.

Program specifications

Program name	INVREG		Page	1
Program description	Prepare invoice register		Date	11/20/96

Input/output specifications

File name	Description	Format	Use
CUST	Customer table	DB2 table	Input
INV	Invoice table	DB2 table	Input
PRTOUT	Invoice register	Print file	Output

Processing specifications

- This program prints an invoice register from the data that it gets from two DB2 tables. These tables are joined by customer number, and one line is printed on the register for each row in the invoice table.

- The first five columns in the invoice register are derived from the INV table; the last two columns are derived from the CUST table; and the sixth column is customer number, which is found in both tables. There are no duplicate customer numbers in the CUST table.

Sample invoice register

```
INVOICE REGISTER - 06/27/97                                                 PAGE:      1

INVOICE    SUBTOTAL       TAX     SHIPPING       TOTAL   CUSTOMER
062308       200.00      0.00        4.45       204.45   400012   S D            HOEHN
062309        15.00      0.00        0.00        15.00   400011   WILLIAM C      FERGUSON
062310       140.00      0.00        7.50       147.50   400011   WILLIAM C      FERGUSON
062311       178.23      0.00        3.19       181.42   400014   R              BINDER
062312       162.00      0.00       11.07       173.07   400002   ARREN          ANELLI
062313        22.00      0.00        0.50        22.50   400011   WILLIAM C      FERGUSON
062314       140.00      9.80        0.00       149.80   400003   SUSAN          HOWARD
062315       178.23      0.00        3.19       181.42   400004   CAROL ANN      EVANS
062316       140.00      0.00        7.50       147.50   400010   ENRIQUE        OTHON
062317       289.00      0.00        9.00       298.00   400011   WILLIAM C      FERGUSON
062318       199.99      0.00        0.00       199.99   400012   S D            HOEHN
062319       178.23      0.00        3.19       181.42   400015   VIVIAN         GEORGE
062320      3245.00      0.00      160.00      3405.00   400015   VIVIAN         GEORGE
062321       200.00      0.00        5.60       205.60   400001   KEITH          MCDONALD
062322        15.00      0.00        0.00        15.00   400014   R              BINDER
062323       925.00      0.00       24.00       949.00   400011   WILLIAM C      FERGUSON
062324       178.23      0.00        3.19       181.42   400014   R              BINDER
062325       140.00      0.00        7.50       147.50   400002   ARREN          ANELLI
062326       178.23      0.00        3.19       181.42   400011   WILLIAM C      FERGUSON
062327       200.00     14.00        7.50       221.50   400003   SUSAN          HOWARD
062328       178.23      0.00        3.19       181.42   400004   CAROL ANN      EVANS
062329       140.00      0.00        7.50       147.50   400010   ENRIQUE        OTHON
062330      2295.00      0.00       14.00      2309.00   400011   WILLIAM C      FERGUSON
062331       178.23      0.00        0.00       178.23   400012   S D            HOEHN
062332       178.23      0.00        0.00       178.23   400013   DAVID R        KEITH
062333       178.23      0.00        0.00       178.23   400015   VIVIAN         GEORGE

TOTALS:    10072.06     23.80      285.26     10381.12          26 INVOICES ISSUED
```

DCLGEN output for the CUST table

```
******************************************************************
* DCLGEN TABLE(MMADBV.CUST)                                      *
*        LIBRARY(MMA002.DCLGENS.COBOL(CUST))                     *
*        ACTION(REPLACE)                                         *
*        STRUCTURE(CUSTOMER-ROW)                                 *
*        APOST                                                   *
* ... IS THE DCLGEN COMMAND THAT MADE THE FOLLOWING STATEMENTS   *
******************************************************************
       EXEC SQL DECLARE MMADBV.CUST TABLE
       ( CUSTNO                          CHAR(6) NOT NULL,
         FNAME                           CHAR(20) NOT NULL,
         LNAME                           CHAR(30) NOT NULL,
         ADDR                            CHAR(30) NOT NULL,
         CITY                            CHAR(20) NOT NULL,
         STATE                           CHAR(2) NOT NULL,
         ZIPCODE                         CHAR(10) NOT NULL
       ) END-EXEC.
******************************************************************
* COBOL DECLARATION FOR TABLE MMADBV.CUST                        *
******************************************************************
  01   CUSTOMER-ROW.
       10 CUSTNO              PIC X(6).
       10 FNAME               PIC X(20).
       10 LNAME               PIC X(30).
       10 ADDR                PIC X(30).
       10 CITY                PIC X(20).
       10 STATE               PIC X(2).
       10 ZIPCODE             PIC X(10).
******************************************************************
* THE NUMBER OF COLUMNS DESCRIBED BY THIS DECLARATION IS 7       *
******************************************************************
```

DCLGEN output for the INV table

```
*********************************************************************
* DCLGEN TABLE(MMADBV.INV)                                          *
*        LIBRARY(MMA002.DCLGENS.COBOL(INV))                         *
*        ACTION(REPLACE)                                            *
*        STRUCTURE(INVOICE-ROW)                                     *
*        APOST                                                      *
* ... IS THE DCLGEN COMMAND THAT MADE THE FOLLOWING STATEMENTS      *
*********************************************************************
      EXEC SQL DECLARE MMADBV.INV TABLE
      ( INVCUST                      CHAR(6) NOT NULL,
        INVNO                        CHAR(6) NOT NULL,
        INVDATE                      DATE NOT NULL,
        INVSUBT                      DECIMAL(9, 2) NOT NULL,
        INVSHIP                      DECIMAL(7, 2) NOT NULL,
        INVTAX                       DECIMAL(7, 2) NOT NULL,
        INVTOTAL                     DECIMAL(9, 2) NOT NULL,
        INVPROM                      CHAR(10) NOT NULL
      ) END-EXEC.
*********************************************************************
* COBOL DECLARATION FOR TABLE MMADBV.INV                            *
*********************************************************************
  01   INVOICE-ROW.
      10 INVCUST           PIC X(6).
      10 INVNO             PIC X(6).
      10 INVDATE           PIC X(10).
      10 INVSUBT           PIC S9999999V99 USAGE COMP-3.
      10 INVSHIP           PIC S99999V99 USAGE COMP-3.
      10 INVTAX            PIC S99999V99 USAGE COMP-3.
      10 INVTOTAL          PIC S9999999V99 USAGE COMP-3.
      10 INVPROM           PIC X(10).
*********************************************************************
* THE NUMBER OF COLUMNS DESCRIBED BY THIS DECLARATION IS 8          *
*********************************************************************
```

The structure chart

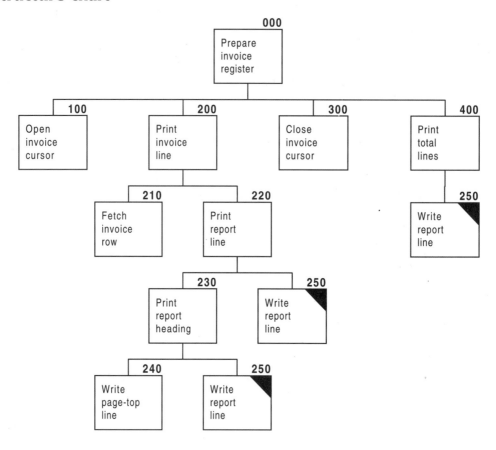

Notes

- Only three of the modules in this structure chart pertain to DB2 processing. Module 100 opens the cursor for the invoice table; module 210 fetches each invoice row; and module 300 closes the cursor for the invoice table. This is consistent with the principle that each I/O operation should be coded in a separate module.
- The other modules show how standard report preparation modules and code can be reused from one program to the next.

Source listing notes

Working-Storage Section

- The SQL INCLUDE statements for CUST and INV are equivalent to COPY statements. They tell the DB2 precompiler to include the descriptions of the tables (the host structures) in the source listing.

- The third INCLUDE statement includes the description of the SQL Communication Area in the source listing. This includes a description of SQLCODE, the field that can be tested after each DB2 operation to determine whether it was successful.

- The fourth SQL statement in Working Storage declares the cursor for the results table described by the SELECT component of this statement. Because this SELECT component returns a multi-row results table, it has to be coded within the DECLARE CURSOR statement.

Modules 100, 210, and 300

- To understand the coding in these modules, you need to know these SQLCODE values: zero (0) indicates a successful operation; +100 indicates that the row hasn't been found or that you've reached the end of a cursor-controlled results table.

Source listing

```
 IDENTIFICATION DIVISION.
*
 PROGRAM-ID.      INVREG.
*
 ENVIRONMENT DIVISION.
*
 INPUT-OUTPUT SECTION.
*
 FILE-CONTROL.
*
     SELECT PRTOUT ASSIGN TO UT-S-PRTOUT.
*
 DATA DIVISION.
*
 FILE SECTION.
*
 FD  PRTOUT
     LABEL RECORDS ARE STANDARD
     BLOCK CONTAINS O RECORDS
     RECORD CONTAINS 132 CHARACTERS.
*
 01  PRTOUT-RECORD                    PIC X(132).
*
 WORKING-STORAGE SECTION.
*
 01  SWITCHES.
*
     05  VALID-CURSOR-SW     PIC X       VALUE "Y".
         88  VALID-CURSOR                VALUE "Y".
     05  END-OF-INVOICES-SW  PIC X       VALUE "N".
         88  END-OF-INVOICES             VALUE "Y".
*
 01  DATE-FIELDS.
*
     05  PRESENT-DATE        PIC 9(6).
     05  PRESENT-DATE-X      REDEFINES PRESENT-DATE.
         10  PRESENT-YEAR    PIC 99.
         10  PRESENT-MONTH   PIC 99.
         10  PRESENT-DAY     PIC 99.
*
 01  INVOICE-TOTAL-FIELDS    COMP-3.
*
     05  INVOICES-COUNT      PIC S9(9)    VALUE ZERO.
     05  INVOICES-SUBTOTAL   PIC S9(9)V99 VALUE ZERO.
     05  INVOICES-TAX        PIC S9(7)V99 VALUE ZERO.
     05  INVOICES-SHIPPING   PIC S9(7)V99 VALUE ZERO
     05  INVOICES-TOTAL      PIC S9(9)V99 VALUE ZERO.
*
 01  PRINT-FIELDS            COMP-3.
*
     05  PAGE-COUNT          PIC S9(5)    VALUE ZERO.
     05  LINE-COUNT          PIC S9(3)    VALUE +999.
     05  LINES-ON-PAGE       PIC S9(3)    VALUE +50.
     05  SPACE-CONTROL       PIC S9(3)    VALUE +1.
*
 01  HEADING-LINE-1.
*
     05  FILLER     PIC X(19)    VALUE "INVOICE REGISTER - ".
     05  HL1-MONTH  PIC XX.
```

```
            05  FILLER      PIC X           VALUE "/".
            05  HL1-DAY     PIC XX.
            05  FILLER      PIC X           VALUE "/".
            05  HL1-YEAR    PIC XX.
            05  FILLER      PIC X(89)       VALUE SPACE.
            05  FILLER      PIC X(6)        VALUE "PAGE: ".
            05  HL1-PAGE    PIC Z(4)9.
            05  FILLER      PIC X(5)        VALUE SPACE.
     *
        01  HEADING-LINE-2.
     *
            05  FILLER      PIC X(20)       VALUE "INVOICE      SUBTOTAL".
            05  FILLER      PIC X(20)       VALUE "        TAX      SHIP".
            05  FILLER      PIC X(20)       VALUE "PING         TOTAL   ".
            05  FILLER      PIC X(20)       VALUE "CUSTOMER             ".
            05  FILLER      PIC X(20)       VALUE "                     ".
            05  FILLER      PIC X(20)       VALUE "                     ".
            05  FILLER      PIC X(12)       VALUE "             ".
     *
        01  REPORT-LINE.
     *
            05  RL-INVNO    PIC X(6).
            05  FILLER      PIC XX          VALUE SPACE.
            05  RL-SUBTOTAL PIC Z(8)9.99.
            05  FILLER      PIC XX          VALUE SPACE.
            05  RL-TAX      PIC Z(6)9.99.
            05  FILLER      PIC XX          VALUE SPACE.
            05  RL-SHIPPING PIC Z(6)9.99.
            05  FILLER      PIC XX          VALUE SPACE.
            05  RL-TOTAL    PIC Z(8)9.99.
            05  FILLER      PIC XX          VALUE SPACE.
            05  RL-CUSTNO   PIC X(6).
            05  FILLER      PIC XX          VALUE SPACE.
            05  RL-FNAME    PIC X(20).
            05  FILLER      PIC XX          VALUE SPACE.
            05  RL-LNAME    PIC X(30).
            05  FILLER      PIC X(12)       VALUE SPACE.
     *
        01  TOTAL-LINE.
     *
            05  FILLER      PIC X(8)        VALUE "TOTALS: ".
            05  TL-SUBTOTAL PIC Z(8)9.99.
            05  FILLER      PIC XX          VALUE SPACE.
            05  TL-TAX      PIC Z(6)9.99.
            05  FILLER      PIC XX          VALUE SPACE.
            05  TL-SHIPPING PIC Z(6)9.99.
            05  FILLER      PIC XX          VALUE SPACE.
            05  TL-TOTAL    PIC Z(8)9.99.
            05  FILLER      PIC XX          VALUE SPACE.
            05  TL-COUNT    PIC Z(8)9.
            05  FILLER      PIC X(16)       VALUE " INVOICES ISSUED".
            05  FILLER      PIC X(47)       VALUE SPACE.
     *
            EXEC SQL
                INCLUDE CUST
            END-EXEC.
     *
            EXEC SQL
                INCLUDE INV
            END-EXEC.
     *
```

```
        EXEC SQL
            INCLUDE SQLCA
        END-EXEC.
*
        EXEC SQL
            DECLARE INVCURS CURSOR FOR
                SELECT    INVNO,    INVSUBT, INVTAX, INVSHIP
                          INVTOTAL, CUSTNO,  FNAME,  LNAME
                    FROM  MMADBV.INV, MMADBV.CUST
                    WHERE INVCUST = CUSTNO
                    ORDER BY INVNO
        END-EXEC.
*
    PROCEDURE DIVISION.
*
    000-PREPARE-INVOICE-REGISTER.
*
        OPEN OUTPUT PRTOUT.
        ACCEPT PRESENT-DATE FROM DATE.
        MOVE PRESENT-MONTH TO HL1-MONTH.
        MOVE PRESENT-DAY   TO HL1-DAY.
        MOVE PRESENT-YEAR  TO HL1-YEAR.
        PERFORM 100-OPEN-INVOICE-CURSOR.
        IF VALID-CURSOR
            PERFORM 200-PRINT-INVOICE-LINE
                UNTIL END-OF-INVOICES
            PERFORM 300-CLOSE-INVOICE-CURSOR.
        PERFORM 400-PRINT-TOTAL-LINES.
        CLOSE PRTOUT.
        STOP RUN.
*
    100-OPEN-INVOICE-CURSOR.
*
        EXEC SQL
            OPEN INVCURS
        END-EXEC.
        IF SQLCODE NOT = 0
            MOVE "N" TO VALID-CURSOR-SW.
*
    200-PRINT-INVOICE-LINE.
*
        PERFORM 210-FETCH-INVOICE-ROW.
        IF NOT END-OF-INVOICES
            IF VALID-CURSOR
                ADD 1            TO INVOICES-COUNT
                ADD INVSUBT      TO INVOICES-SUBTOTAL
                ADD INVTAX       TO INVOICES-TAX
                ADD INVSHIP      TO INVOICES-SHIPPING
                ADD INVTOTAL     TO INVOICES-TOTAL
                MOVE INVNO       TO RL-INVNO
                MOVE INVSUBT     TO RL-SUBTOTAL
                MOVE INVTAX      TO RL-TAX
                MOVE INVSHIP     TO RL-SHIPPING
                MOVE INVTOTAL    TO RL-TOTAL
                MOVE CUSTNO      TO RL-CUSTNO
                MOVE FNAME       TO RL-FNAME
                MOVE LNAME       TO RL-LNAME
                PERFORM 220-PRINT-REPORT-LINE.
```

```
*
 210-FETCH-INVOICE-ROW.
*
     EXEC SQL
         FETCH INVCURS
             INTO :INVNO,      :INVSUBT,   :INVTAX,   :INVSHIP,
                  :INVTOTAL,  :CUSTNO,    :FNAME,    :LNAME
     END-EXEC.
     IF SQLCODE NOT = 0
         MOVE "Y" TO END-OF-INVOICES-SW
         IF SQLCODE NOT = 100
             MOVE "N" TO VALID-CURSOR-SW.
*
 220-PRINT-REPORT-LINE.
*
     IF LINE-COUNT > LINES-ON-PAGE
         PERFORM 230-PRINT-REPORT-HEADING
         MOVE 1 TO LINE-COUNT.
     MOVE REPORT-LINE TO PRTOUT-RECORD.
     PERFORM 250-WRITE-REPORT-LINE.
     ADD 1 TO LINE-COUNT.
     MOVE 1 TO SPACE-CONTROL.
*
 230-PRINT-REPORT-HEADING.
*
     ADD 1 TO PAGE-COUNT.
     MOVE PAGE-COUNT TO HL1-PAGE.
     MOVE HEADING-LINE-1 TO PRTOUT-RECORD.
     PERFORM 240-WRITE-PAGE-TOP-LINE.
     MOVE 2 TO SPACE-CONTROL.
     MOVE HEADING-LINE-2 TO PRTOUT-RECORD.
     PERFORM 250-WRITE-REPORT-LINE.
*
 240-WRITE-PAGE-TOP-LINE.
*
     WRITE PRTOUT-RECORD
         AFTER ADVANCING PAGE.
*
 250-WRITE-REPORT-LINE.
*
     WRITE PRTOUT-RECORD
         AFTER SPACE-CONTROL LINES.
*
 300-CLOSE-INVOICE-CURSOR.
*
     EXEC SQL
         CLOSE INVCURS
     END-EXEC.
     IF SQLCODE NOT = 0
         MOVE "N" TO VALID-CURSOR-SW.
```

```
*
  400-PRINT-TOTAL-LINES.
*
      IF VALID-CURSOR
          MOVE INVOICES-SUBTOTAL TO TL-SUBTOTAL
          MOVE INVOICES-TAX      TO TL-TAX
          MOVE INVOICES-SHIPPING TO TL-SHIPPING
          MOVE INVOICES-TOTAL    TO TL-TOTAL
          MOVE INVOICES-COUNT    TO TL-COUNT
          MOVE TOTAL-LINE        TO PRTOUT-RECORD
      ELSE
          MOVE "****  DB2 ERROR   --  INCOMPLETE REPORT  ****"
                                 TO PRTOUT-RECORD.
      MOVE 2 TO SPACE-CONTROL.
      PERFORM 250-WRITE-REPORT-LINE.
```

Appendix A

To see how easy it is to modify a program that is based on the design and coding principles of this book, try one of the exercises that follow. Each one asks you to make a modification to one of the model programs. Exercises 2 and 3 also show how easy it is to reuse code from one program in another.

When you plan the solutions to these exercises, start by identifying the changes that are required in the structure chart for the program. To do that, you can just mark the changes on the chart in this book or make a copy of the chart and then mark the changes. This should show you how easy it is to determine design changes when you use the methods of this book.

Next, identify the changes that need to be made to the COBOL code. Which modules need to be changed? What changes need to be made in each module? What should the code for the new modules be? The best way to plan those changes is to use pseudocode, and that by itself should show you how easy it is to modify the code in a program when you use the methods in this book.

If you want to actually make and test the changes, you can get the code for the model programs on diskette. This will give you hands-on experience that will help you get comfortable with the methods of this book. It may also remove any lingering doubts you may have about them. For diskette ordering information, please see the last pages of this book.

Exercise 1

Modify model program 1 so the data for each branch is printed on a separate page

Oh, oh, here's a late change to the specifications for this program. Please start the data for each branch on a new page of the report. This will show you how easy it is to make a simple change to a program that follows the guidelines presented in this book...even someone else's program. This change should take about five minutes.

Exercise 2

Create a new program from model program 1 that prepares a sales by salesrep within branch report

Just down from marketing department: "Please prepare a new report for us each month that gives summarized totals by salesrep within branch." This report should print one summary line for each salesrep (no detail lines for customers) and one summary line for each branch. This means the salesrep number and name should replace the customer number and name in the report.

To get the salesrep names, you can use a file named REPMAST with this format:

```
01   SALESREP-MASTER-RECORD.
*
     05   SM-SALESREP-KEY
          10   SM-BRANCH-NUMBER      PIC XX.
          10   SM-SALESREP-NUMBER    PIC XX.
     05   SM-SALESREP-NAME           PIC X(18).
```

The records in this file can be accessed by the salesrep key field.

Since the customer file is already in sequence by customer number within salesrep number within branch number, this shouldn't be much trouble. Note, however, that this isn't a request for a program modification. It's a request for a new program. The best way to prepare this new program is to copy model program 1, rename it, and modify it so it fits the new specifications.

Exercise 3

Modify model program 1 so it prepares a sales by customer within salesrep within branch report

Another request from the marketing department: "Please modify the sales by customer within branch report so it also prints totals for each salesrep." This means the salesrep number and name has to be added to the report (between the branch name and customer number).

To get the salesrep names, you can use the REPMAST file that's described in exercise 2. Better yet, you can copy the code for using that file from the program you created in exercise 2. Or would it be better to start this programming change from the program you create in exercise 2 and then copy some of the code from model program 1 into it? You decide.

Exercise 4

Modify model program 2 so it sorts the transaction records before it processes them

Due to a change in system requirements, your project manager says the transaction records must be sorted into item number sequence before the program uses them to update the inventory master record. This will put them in the proper sequence for processing by subsequent programs; it may also improve processing efficiency.

Exercise 5

Modify model program 2 so it only rewrites a record after all transactions for that record have been processed

Assuming the transactions are in item number sequence, processing efficiency will improve if the program doesn't rewrite a record until all the transactions for each master record have been processed. The way the model program is written now, though, it rewrites an updated master record after each transaction has been processed. What change, if any, must be made to the structure chart for this program modification?

Exercise 6

Modify model program 3 so it gets the customer number from a control file when a new customer record is added to the file

To add a record to the customer master file when you use model program 3, the user has to enter the new customer number. Due to complaints about this procedure, though, you're supposed to modify the program so it derives the number for the next new customer from a control file named CTRLNUMS with this format:

```
01    CONTROL-NUMBERS.
*
      05    CN-LAST-CUSTOMER-NUMBER    PIC  X(6).
      05    CN-LAST-VENDOR-NUMBER      PIC  X(5).
      05    CN-LAST-EMPLOYEE-NUMBER    PIC  X(5).
      05    FILLER                     PIC  X(64).
```

This also affects the interactive coding because the user doesn't include a customer number on the action screen before starting a customer addition.

Appendix B

What our structure listing program does

In our shop, we use a program called LISTMODS to generate a structure listing from a COBOL source program. Then, this structure listing (not the structure chart) becomes the final design documentation for the program. If you like this idea but need a program for this purpose, ours is available at a modest price (see the order form that follows).

The input to LISTMODS is a COBOL source program that's coded using the guidelines presented in this book. The output is a printed structure listing like the one on the facing page. This listing shows the calls to subprograms like 'GETDATE' as well as the calls to COBOL modules, and a C after a name marks a common module.

After the structure listing, the program prints a summary page. This page lists error messages, uncalled modules, called subprograms, and DECLARATIVES (if you've used any). It also prints some program statistics.

Since LISTMODS is a COBOL program that uses 1974 standard code, it can easily be modified to work on any system. Usually, you just need to (1) get the compiler options set right and (2) adjust the SELECT and FD statements so they are appropriate for your system.

It's also easy to make some basic modifications to LISTMODS. If, for example, you want the program to process sections instead of paragraphs, you just change the switch value for PARAGRAPH-MODULES-SW to "N". And if you don't want asterisks (*) to print in the structure listings, you delete the source lines that have AST in columns 73-75.

Once you've got LISTMODS working, you can use it to create a structure listing for its own source code. Then, the complete documentation for LISTMODS consists of its structure listing, its source code, and a small user's guide in the form of a README.DOC that comes with the program.

Since the code for this COBOL program adheres to all the principles presented in this book, you should be able to read and understand its code without too much trouble. Although LISTMODS is certainly not a typical business program, it's interesting to see how this program is designed and coded. Once you understand it, you should be able to modify or enhance its code as you see fit.

The structure listing and statistics for model program 1

```
DATE AND TIME: 01/22/97  11:08 AM                                    PAGE:   1
PROGRAM-ID:    MKTG1200

*
 000-PREPARE-SALES-REPORT
*
     100-FORMAT-REPORT-HEADING
     *
         'GETDATE'
     *
     200-LOAD-BRANCH-TABLE
     *
         210-READ-BRANCH-RECORD
     *
     300-PREPARE-SALES-LINES
     *
         310-READ-CUSTOMER-RECORD
         320-PRINT-CUSTOMER-LINE
         *
             330-SEARCH-BRANCH-TABLE
             340-PRINT-HEADING-LINES
             *
                 350-WRITE-PAGE-TOP-LINE
                 360-WRITE-REPORT-LINE                 C
             *
             360-WRITE-REPORT-LINE                 C
         *
         370-ACCUMULATE-SALES-TOTALS
         380-PRINT-BRANCH-LINE
         *
             360-WRITE-REPORT-LINE                 C
         *
     *
     500-PRINT-GRAND-TOTALS
     *
         360-WRITE-REPORT-LINE             C
     *
```

```
DATE AND TIME: 01/22/97  11:08 AM                                    PAGE:   2
PROGRAM-ID:    MKTG1200

CALLED SUBPROGRAMS ----------------------------------------------------------

'GETDATE'

PROGRAM STATISTICS ----------------------------------------------------------

TOTAL LINES IN PROGRAM:         387
TOTAL LINES MINUS COMMENTS:     312
PD LINES MINUS COMMENTS:        173

NUMBER OF COBOL SECTIONS:         0
NUMBER OF COBOL PARAGRAPHS:      14
NUMBER OF SUBPROGRAMS USED:       1
AVG. LINES PER COBOL MODULE:     12

NUMBER OF PERFORM STATEMENTS:    26
NUMBER OF INLINE PERFORMS:        1
NUMBER OF CALL STATEMENTS:        1
NUMBER OF SORT STATEMENTS:        0
NUMBER OF MERGE STATEMENTS:       0
NO. OF SORT/MERGE PROCEDURES:     0
NUMBER OF GO TO STATEMENTS:       0
```

Index

COBOL products from Mike Murach & Associates

LISTMODS and Model Programs on diskette

Take advantage of all the work Paul Noll's already done, and save yourself hours of program development time with this bargain-priced diskette. You get:

- the COBOL code for the 5 model programs in this book (these make it easy for you to start reusing tested code that you're already familiar with, instead of developing each new program from scratch)

- the COBOL code for the structure listing program, LISTMODS, that's described in Appendix B (this

makes it easy for you to automatically document your new programs)

So stop working so hard! Let this companion diskette help you get the most out of all the time-saving methods you've learned in this book, starting TODAY!

Structured COBOL Methods diskette:
5 model COBOL programs, LISTMODS,
User's Guide for LISTMODS (in text format), **$25.00**

VS COBOL II

2nd Edition   **Anne Prince**

This book builds on your COBOL knowledge to quickly teach you everything you need to know about VS COBOL II, the IBM 1985 COBOL compiler for MVS shops:

- how to code the language elements that are new in VS COBOL II... and what language elements you can't use any more

- CICS considerations

- how to use the debugger

- how the compiler's features can make your programs compile and run more efficiently

- guidelines for converting to VS COBOL II (that includes coverage of the conversion aids IBM supplies)

So if you're in a shop that's already converted to VS COBOL II, you'll learn how to benefit from the language elements and features the compiler has to offer. If you aren't yet working in VS COBOL II, you'll learn how to write programs now that will be easy to convert later on. And if you're a manager, you'll get some practical ideas on when to convert and how to do it as painlessly as possible.

VS COBOL II, 7 chapters, 271 pages, **$27.50**
ISBN 0-911625-54-2

VSAM for the COBOL Programmer

Second Edition   **Doug Lowe**

This short book covers all you need to know to handle VSAM files in your COBOL programs: critical VSAM terms and concepts...the COBOL elements for handling key-sequenced, entry-sequenced, and relative-record VSAM files...how to handle alternate indexes, dynamic access, and error processing...how to use the Access

Method Services utility (AMS)...how to code JCL for VSAM files...how your code is affected if you're working under VS COBOL II.

VSAM for COBOL, 6 chapters, 187 pages, **$22.50**
ISBN 0-911625-45-3

 Call toll-free 1-800-221-5528 • Weekdays, 8-5 Pacific Time • Fax: 1-209-275-9035

CICS books from Mike Murach & Associates

CICS for the COBOL Programmer

Second Edition   **Doug Lowe**

This 2-part course is designed to help COBOL programmers become outstanding CICS programmers.

Part 1: An Introductory Course covers the basic CICS elements you'll use in just about every program you write. So you'll learn about basic mapping support (BMS), pseudo-conversational programming, basic CICS commands, sensible program design using event-driven design techniques, testing and debugging using IBM-supplied transactions (like CEMT, CECI, and CEDF) or a transaction dump, and efficiency considerations.

Part 2: An Advanced Course covers CICS features you'll use regularly, though you won't need all of them for every program. That means you'll learn about browse commands, temporary storage, transient data, data tables (including the shared data table feature of CICS 3.3), DB2 and DL/I processing considerations,

distributed processing features, interval control commands, BMS page building, and more! In addition, *Part 2* teaches you which features do similar things and when to use each one. So you won't just learn how to code new functions...you'll also learn how to choose the best CICS solution for each programming problem you face.

Both books cover all versions of CICS up through 3.3. Both cover OS/VS COBOL, VS COBOL II, and COBOL/370, so it doesn't matter which COBOL compiler you're using. And all the program examples in both books conform to CUA's Entry Model for screen design.

CICS, Part 1, 12 chapters, 409 pages, **$36.50**
ISBN 0-911625-60-7

CICS, Part 2, 12 chapters, 352 pages, **$36.50**
ISBN 0-911625-67-4

The CICS Programmer's Desk Reference

Second Edition   **Doug Lowe**

Ever feel buried by IBM manuals?

It seems like you need stacks of them, close at hand, if you want to be an effective CICS programmer. Because frankly, there's just too much you have to know to do your job well; you can't keep it all in your head.

That's why Doug Lowe decided to write *The CICS Programmer's Desk Reference*. In it, he's collected all the information you need to have at your fingertips, and organized it into 12 sections that make it easy for you to find what you're looking for. So there are sections on:

- BMS macro instructions—their formats (with an explanation of each parameter) and coding examples

- CICS commands—their syntax (with an explanation of each parameter), coding examples, and suggestions on how and when to use each one most effectively

- MVS and DOS/VSE JCL for CICS applications

- AMS commands for handling VSAM files

- details for MVS users on how to use ISPF

- complete model programs, including specs, design, and code

- a summary of CICS program design techniques that lead to simple, maintainable, and efficient programs

- guidelines for testing and debugging CICS applications

- and more!

So clear the IBM manuals off your terminal table. Let the *Desk Reference* be your everyday guide to CICS instead.

CICS Desk Reference, 12 sections, 507 pages, **$42.50**
ISBN 0-911625-68-2

 Call toll-free 1-800-221-5528 • Weekdays, 8-5 Pacific Time • Fax: 1-209-275-9035

DB2 books from Mike Murach & Associates

DB2 for the COBOL Programmer

Part 1: An Introductory Course   **Steve Eckols**

If you're looking for a practical DB2 book that focuses on application programming, this is the book for you. Written from the programmer's point of view, it will quickly teach you what you need to know to access and process DB2 data in your COBOL programs using embedded SQL. You'll learn:

- what DB2 is and how it works, so you'll have the background you need to program more easily and logically

- how to design and code application programs that retrieve and update DB2 data

- how to use basic error handling and data integrity techniques to protect DB2 data

- how to use joins and unions to combine data from two or more tables into a single table

- how to use DB2 column functions to extract summary information from a table

- how to use a subquery or subselect when one SQL statement depends on the results of another

- how to work with variable-length data and nulls

- how to develop DB2 programs interactively (using DB2I, a TSO facility) or in batch

So if you want to learn how to write DB2 application programs, get a copy of this book today!

DB2, Part 1, 11 chapters, 371 pages, **$36.50**
ISBN 0-911625-59-3

DB2 for the COBOL Programmer

Part 2: An Advanced Course   **Steve Eckols**

Once you've mastered the basics of DB2 programming, there's still plenty to learn. So this book teaches you all the advanced DB2 features that will make you a more capable programmer...and shows you when to use each one. You'll learn:

- how to use advanced data manipulation and error handling techniques

- how to use dynamic SQL

- how to work with distributed DB2 data

- how to maximize locking efficiency and concurrency to maintain the accuracy of DB2 data even while a number of programs have access to that data

- how to access and process DB2 data in CICS programs

- what you need to know about data base administration so you can design and define your own tables for program testing (this will make you a more productive and professional programmer, even if you never want to be a DBA)

- how to use QMF, IBM's Query Management Facility, to issue SQL statements interactively and to prepare formatted reports

So don't wait to expand your DB2 skills. Get a copy of this book TODAY.

DB2, Part 2, 15 chapters, 393 pages, **$36.50**
ISBN 0-911625-64-X

 Call toll-free 1-800-221-5528 • Weekdays, 8-5 Pacific Time • Fax: 1-209-275-9035

DL/I and IMS books from Mike Murach & Associates

IMS for the COBOL Programmer

Part 1: DL/I Data Base Processing   **Steve Eckols**

This how-to book will have you writing batch DL/I programs in a minimum of time—whether you're working on a VSE or an MVS system. But it doesn't neglect the conceptual background you must have to create programs that work. So you'll learn:

- what a DL/I data base is and how its data elements are organized into a hierarchical structure
- the COBOL elements for creating, accessing, and updating DL/I data bases...including logical data bases and data bases with secondary indexing
- how to use DL/I recovery and restart features
- the basic DL/I considerations for coding interactive programs using IMS/DC or CICS

- how data bases with the 4 common types of DL/I data base organizations are stored (this material will help you program more logically and efficiently for the type of data base you're using)
- and more!

7 complete COBOL programs show you how to process DL/I data bases in various ways. Use them as models for production work in your shop, and you'll save hours of development time.

IMS, Part 1, 16 chapters, 333 pages, **$36.50**
ISBN 0-911625-29-1

IMS for the COBOL Programmer

Part 2: Data Communications and Message Format Service   **Steve Eckols**

The second part of *IMS for the COBOL Programmer* is for MVS programmers only. It teaches how to develop online programs that access IMS data bases and run under the data communications (DC) component of IMS. So you'll learn:

- why you code message processing programs (MPPs) the way you do (DC programs are called MPPs because they process messages sent from and to user terminals)
- what COBOL elements you use for MPPs
- how to use Message Format Service (MFS), a facility for formatting complex terminal displays so you can enhance the look and operation of your DC programs
- how to develop applications that use more than one screen format or that use physical and logical paging

- how to develop batch message processing (BMP) programs to update IMS data bases in batch even while they're being used by other programs
- how to use Batch Terminal Simulator (BTS) to test DC applications using IMS resources, but without disrupting the everyday IMS processing that's going on
- and more!

8 complete programs—including MFS format sets, program design, and COBOL code—show you how to handle various DC and MFS applications. Use them as models to save yourself hours of coding and debugging.

IMS, Part 2, 16 chapters, 398 pages, **$36.50**
ISBN 0-911625-30-5

 Call toll-free 1-800-221-5528 • Weekdays, 8-5 Pacific Time • Fax: 1-209-275-9035

Comment Form

Your opinions count

If you have any comments, criticisms, or suggestions for us, I'm eager to hear from you. Your opinions today will affect our products of tomorrow. And if you find any errors in this book, typographical or otherwise, please point them out so we can correct them in the next printing.

Thanks for your help.

Mike Murach

Book title: Structured COBOL Methods

Dear Mike: _____

_____

_____

_____

_____

_____

_____

_____

_____

_____

_____

_____

_____

_____

_____

Name _____

Company (if company address) _____

Address _____

City, State, Zip _____

Fold where indicated and tape closed.
No postage needed if mailed in the U.S.

BUSINESS REPLY MAIL

FIRST-CLASS MAIL   PERMIT NO. 3063   FRESNO, CA

POSTAGE WILL BE PAID BY ADDRESSEE

Mike Murach & Associates, Inc.

2560 W SHAW LN STE 101
FRESNO CA 93711-9866

Order Form

Our Unlimited Guarantee

To our customers who order directly from us: You must be satisfied. Our books must work for you, or you can send them back for a full refund...no questions asked.

Name & Title _____

Company (if company address) _____

Street Address _____

City, State, Zip _____

Phone number (including area code) _____

Fax number (if you fax your order to us) _____

Qty	Product code and title	*Price
COBOL programming		
___ SCMD	Structured COBOL Methods	$25.00
___ SCDK	Structured COBOL Methods diskette (5 model programs + LISTMODS)	25.00
___ VC2R	VS COBOL II (Second Edition)	27.50
___ SC1R	Structured ANS COBOL, Part 1	32.50
___ SC2R	Structured ANS COBOL, Part 2	32.50
CICS		
___ CC1R	CICS for the COBOL Programmer Part 1 (Second Edition)	$36.50
___ CC2R	CICS for the COBOL Programmer Part 2 (Second Edition)	36.50
___ CRFR	The CICS Programmer's Desk Reference (Second Edition)	42.50
VSAM		
___ VSMX	VSAM: Access Method Services and Application Programming	$27.50
___ VSMR	VSAM for the COBOL Programmer (Second Edition)	22.50

Qty	Product code and title	*Price
Data Base Processing		
___ DB21	DB2 for the COBOL Programmer Part 1: An Introductory Course	$36.50
___ DB22	DB2 for the COBOL Programmer Part 2: An Advanced Course	36.50
___ IMS1	IMS for the COBOL Programmer Part 1: DL/I Data Base Processing	36.50
___ IMS2	IMS for the COBOL Programmer Part 2: Data Communications and MFS	36.50
MVS Subjects		
___ MJLR	MVS JCL (Second Edition)	$42.50
___ TSO1	MVS TSO, Part 1: Concepts and ISPF	36.50
___ TSO2	MVS TSO, Part 2: Commands and Procedures (CLIST and REXX)	36.50
___ MBAL	MVS Assembler Language	36.50
DOS/VSE Subjects		
___ VJLR	DOS/VSE JCL (Second Edition)	$34.50
___ ICCF	DOS/VSE ICCF	31.00
___ VBAL	VSE Assembler Language	36.50

❑ Bill me for the books plus UPS shipping and handling (and sales tax within California).

❑ Bill my company. P.O.# _____

❑ I want to **SAVE 10%** by paying in advance. Charge to my ___Visa ___MasterCard ___American Express:

Card number _____

Valid thru (mo/yr) _____

Cardowner's signature _____

❑ I want to **SAVE 10% plus shipping and handling.** Here's my check or money order for the books minus 10% ($_____). California residents, please add sales tax to your total. (Offer valid in U.S.)

*Prices are subject to change. Please call for current prices.

To order more quickly,

Call **toll-free** 1-800-221-5528

(Weekdays, 8 to 5 Pacific Time)

Fax: 1-209-275-9035

Mike Murach & Associates, Inc.

2560 West Shaw Lane, Suite 101
Fresno, California 93711-2765
(209) 275-3335

NO POSTAGE
NECESSARY
IF MAILED
IN THE
UNITED STATES

BUSINESS REPLY MAIL

FIRST-CLASS MAIL   PERMIT NO. 3063   FRESNO, CA

POSTAGE WILL BE PAID BY ADDRESSEE

Mike Murach & Associates, Inc.

2560 W SHAW LN STE 101
FRESNO CA 93711-9866